Cambridge Topics in Geography : second series

Editors: Alan R. H. Baker, Emmanuel College, Cambridge
Colin Evans, King's College School, Wimbledon

South American development
A geographical introduction

Rosemary D. F. Bromley
Department of Geography, University College of Swansea

Ray Bromley
Department of Geography and Planning,
State University of New York at Albany

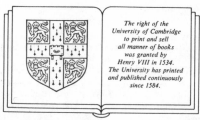

The right of the
University of Cambridge
to print and sell
all manner of books
was granted by
Henry VIII in 1534.
The University has printed
and published continuously
since 1584.

Cambridge University Press
Cambridge
New York   Port Chester   Melbourne   Sydney

Published by the Press Syndicate of the University of Cambridge
The Pitt Building, Trumpington Street, Cambridge CB2 1RP
40 West 20th Street, New York, NY 10011, USA
10 Stamford Road, Oakleigh, Melbourne 3166, Australia

First published 1982
Reprinted 1985
Second edition 1988
Reprinted 1989

Printed in Great Britain at the the University Press, Cambridge

Library of Congress catalogue card number : 88-16216

British Library cataloguing in publication data

Bromley, Rosemary D. F.
 South American development : a geographical
 introduction.—2nd ed.—(Cambridge topics
 in geography. Second series)
 1. South America. Geographical features
 I. Title   II. Bromley, Ray
 918

 ISBN 0 521 36727 1
 (First edition ISBN 0 521 23496 hard covers
 ISBN 0 521 28008 7 paperback)

Acknowledgements

We are grateful to Dr G. Williams for supplying Fig. 2.7, to Mr C. Dumeuil for
Fig. 6.11 and to Dr G. Humphrys for Fig. 7.3. The remaining photographs, taken by
the authors, were prepared by the Photographic Unit of the Department of
Geography, University College of Swansea, where we particularly wish to acknowledge
the assistance of Mr A. Cutliffe. Our manuscript was efficiently typed by Mrs D. E.
Ashworth, Miss J. Lovell, Mrs D. Slater and Mrs A. Thomas, and photocopied by Mr
J. Rusque. Mr T. Fearnside, in the Cartographic Unit, Department of Geography,
University College of Swansea drew Fig. 5.9. Thanks are due to the following for
permission to derive and reproduce maps and diagrams: Fig. 2.3 H. Blackmore (Ed.),
Latin America, British Broadcasting Corporation, 1974; (2.8) G. Pendle, *Argentina*,
Royal Institute of International Affairs, 1955; (2.6) R. Graham, *Britain and the onset
of modernization in Brazil, 1850–1914*, Cambridge University Press, 1968.

Contents

Preface

This book has been written with two major objectives. The first is to provide a systematic human geography text on South America, concentrating on themes and issues rather than on the presentation of detailed factual information on specific countries and regions. The second objective is to introduce and develop a welfare approach, and through this to inject an element of political economy into geographical teaching on South America. The focus is upon those factors which influence the distribution of wealth and poverty, and in particular their close spatial juxtaposition within the same continent. These factors are analysed through an examination of the different interpretations of 'development' as applied to the five main subject areas discussed in this volume: the legacy of the past, agrarian problems and dilemmas, industrialization, urbanization, and resource exploitation. For each of these subject areas the emphasis is on social and economic inequalities, their causes, and the ways in which the distribution and extent of inequality change through time.

This is an introductory text which seeks to present the issues as simply and coherently as possible, while at the same time ensuring the necessary brevity. We assume no more than the most basic knowledge of geographical, social, economic and political concepts, so that the book will appeal to a wide readership. We have deliberately limited the range of concepts we cover and have explained each of them as they arise.

South America has a distinctive place in the Third World: not only because of its history and culture, but because its poverty is less pronounced than in the other Third World continents. It is further along the road of economic growth than most of Africa or South and South-East Asia, yet it still features great internal inequalities. By providing some familiarity with the fundamental issues in South American development, we seek to stimulate interest, to raise questions, to motivate further reading, and to provide a link between academic learning and the events discussed in current affairs broadcasting, magazines and newspapers. Hopefully, when there is a new coup d'etat in Bolivia, an earthquake in Peru, or a major trading agreement between Venezuela and West Germany, the reader will be aware of the range of causes and effects, and of those who might benefit, and of those who might suffer. We wish to draw the reader's attention to the range of different viewpoints and to encourage a vision of South America as something more than a continent of spectacular scenery, commodity production and Latin ways.

This book was written at the University College of Swansea, where we benefited immensely from informal discussions with the academics and students of the Department of Geography and the Centre for Development Studies. We are grateful for their assistance, and indebted to the series editors for their advice. This second, revised, edition has been prepared while we are on different sides of the Atlantic. Like the first edition, it is dedicated to our son Martin.

Rosemary D. F. Bromley and Ray Bromley
Swansea and Albany, 1988

1 What is development?

In human geography, and in such other social sciences as economics, politics, sociology and anthropology, the term 'development' is used to refer to any process of gradual, long-term change in the conditions affecting human life. Such changes are mainly the result of human decisions and actions. Powerful individuals, organizations, companies and governments can all have major influences on the development process. No one, however, has total power to bring about whatever changes are desired. The possibilities for human action are always limited by the shortages of available resources, the effects of past actions, and the problems and potential which people see in their natural environments.

The long-term changes which occur in the conditions affecting human life are made up of sequences of events and short-term changes which combine to produce a general trend. When no long-term trend exists, there is no development taking place, and we generally talk of stability or stagnation. When conditions are changing in a way that is clearly opposite to the general trend, we can talk of a transition, depression, or crisis. This may lead to a resumption of the original trend and development process, or to a major upheaval and the start of an entirely new trend and development process. Those areas which have been more affected by long-term change can be described as 'more developed', and those which have been less affected as 'less developed' or 'underdeveloped'. The term 'underdeveloped' can suggest either a relative absence of development, or some process of change which is opposite to the long-term changes described as development.

Development, therefore, is a process of change over a period of time which can be studied by anyone with a historical interest, and which can sometimes be predicted by forecasters. It can be strongly influenced by human actions designed to change future conditions, and so it is of particular concern to political leaders, administrators and planners. Many geographers are also concerned with history, politics and planning, and hence have an interest in the study of development. However, there are three more important reasons why the study of development is central to geography. The first is that contrasting areas sometimes undergo different sorts of development or experience different rates of development. Geographers are able to use their skills in examining the spatial patterns of development and the ways in which these patterns change through time. Secondly, the geographer is interested in the interrelationships between people and their environment. The geographer is therefore aware of the ways in which the environment can restrict change and also of the potential it offers. The third reason is the geographer's interest in the unequal distribution of wealth and poverty around the world. The value of any study of this distribution is greatly increased by an understanding of how the present day inequalities arose. These three reasons relate directly to the three major areas of concern in modern human geography: the study of spatial patterns and how they change through time, the study of man–environment relations and the study of the processes causing spatial inequalities.

'Development' and 'underdevelopment' are the two words most frequently used to describe the distribution of wealth and poverty around the world. Despite the fact that development suggests long-term change, and underdevelopment suggests the relative absence or bad effects of such change, each of the two words has several different meanings and implications. People often use the words in different ways at different times. Our aim in this first chapter is to explain their different meanings. After this explanation, readers will be able to consider each topic in terms of the types of development which are taking place and the extent to which development is benefiting different groups of the population. They can also assess the degree to which underdevelopment is being reduced, or is actually increasing, as a result of the development process.

Development as improvement

The simplest concept of development is the idea of progress or improvement. In any real situation, however, it is unlikely that everyone involved will agree on what is progress or improvement. Some will view particular changes as development, while others will see them as backward steps. For example, in every society there are changes in fashions for clothes, music and entertainment. Some people lead in making these changes, others follow, some ignore them, and others may actually resist the changes and do what they consider to be the opposite. Each of these groups sees the whole process of change differently. Some favour change and consider it progress. Some have no interest in the changes which are taking place and feel that these are not leading anywhere. Others actively oppose the changes and consider them retrogressive.

Different reactions to changes in clothes, music and entertainment may reflect no more than differences in age, in background and upbringing. Often though, the question of whether a particular change is viewed as progress depends on a person's political, moral or religious beliefs. Hence different political parties, interest groups and religious denominations can disagree about what development actually is in a particular context. When such disagreements occur, a fair solution might be to hold an election on the issues involved, and to allow everyone to vote, in the hope of defining a majority view. Even in countries with regular elections, however, they are relatively infrequent, and the people who vote do not necessarily have a clear understanding of the election issues. In some countries there are dictatorships and no elections. In others the elections are arranged by those who already have power, so that the result is a foregone conclusion, or there is a one-party state where there is no real choice at election time. Finally, some countries of the world are still ruled from outside. Even if these countries are not colonies, their governments can be under pressure from powerful foreign governments, large foreign companies or international banks. Therefore when differences of opinion occur about what is an improvement, the majority opinion is often not as important as that of the most powerful interest group, even if that interest group is relatively small in numbers.

The variety of views on whether particular changes are improvements, and can therefore be defined as development, is illustrated by an example from Brazil. Since 1976, there have been many discussions about the

Fig. 1.1 A nuclear power station under construction in South-East Brazil. Such modern sources of power require massive investments, and also considerable technical assistance from the First World (see page 17).

Brazilian government's expensive nuclear energy generation programme, which was started with technical help from West Germany. This programme is supported by the army because it is considered to improve national security, helping the country to become self-sufficient in energy, and eventually to manufacture nuclear weapons. Many industrialists also support the programme because they are likely to benefit by getting contracts to supply materials or to make the necessary equipment. Those involved in trade and other contacts with West Germany also approve of the programme. All of these interest groups see nuclear power as the energy source of the future, and consider that the nuclear programme will enable Brazil to join the ranks of the world's wealthiest countries. Other interest groups, however, argue that Brazil has one of the greatest potentials in the world for hydroelectricity, and that such energy can be generated more quickly and cheaply than nuclear energy. They suggest that the nuclear power programme is diverting scarce government money

Fig. 1.2 An itinerant drinking-water seller in the town of Mossoró in North-East Brazil. The water is carried in the large barrel fixed to the horse-drawn cart. Many of the poorer inhabitants have no piped water supply to their homes. This contrasts markedly with the high technology employed in nuclear power generation.

away from more useful projects, and that the programme is wasting resources and increasing Brazil's reliance on foreign assistance. Some go on to point out the dangers of nuclear fall-out. Others suggest that in a country where there is still malnutrition, illiteracy and ill-health amongst the poor, energy production is receiving far too much government money and only benefiting the better-off members of the population (Figs. 1.1 and 1.2). Thus, what is certainly an improvement for some interest groups is viewed as a wasteful step by others. The important point which arises from the Brazilian example is that any definition of development in terms of progress or improvement reflects a value judgment by the people who assess the situation. They base their judgment on their own knowledge and views, and others may well come to a different judgment because they come with different knowledge and views.

Development as growth

The best-known theories of development are linked with the study of economic development, and particularly with national rates of economic growth. To many economists, development has come to be associated more with growth than with any concept of progress. Some actually argue that economic growth always means progress and always brings benefits, because it creates more wealth. This wealth might then be redistributed amongst the population so that everyone is better off.

Economic growth takes place when there is an increase in a country's total output. This is usually measured by the rate of growth of Gross Domestic Product (GDP), or Gross National Product (GNP). GDP comprises the total value of goods and services produced within a country in a particular year. GNP is GDP plus any income received from investments abroad, less similar income earned by those abroad who have invested in the country. In poor countries, the income gained from investments abroad is usually less than the payments made to foreigners investing in those countries. In these cases, GNP is slightly less than GDP. In the richer countries, where a large income is earned from investments abroad, GNP is usually a little greater than GDP.

When GDP (or GNP) grows, it can typically increase in size from one year to the next by as little as 1 per cent, or by as much as 10 per cent. On its own, however, a growth in GDP in real terms (i.e. removing the effects of inflation on prices) does not tell us whether the average person is better off. There may also have been a growth in population which reduces or even reverses the effect of the growth in GDP. For example, if GDP grows by only 2 per cent over the year, while population grows by 3 per cent, there is a slight decline (about 1 per cent) in GDP per capita. For this reason, economic growth is usually only said to have taken place if the growth in GDP exceeds the growth in population, or in other words, if there has been an increase in GDP per capita. As population growth in most countries is less than 3½ per cent per annum, we can generally assume that any rates of growth in GDP over that amount will produce increases in GDP per capita.

When a country experiences a growth in GDP or GNP per capita, economic growth is taking place and the average person both produces and consumes a little more each year than in previous years. If everyone were average, everyone would be better off materially and financially and almost everyone would feel that growth is good. Under such circumstances, the only obvious argument against growth might be that it increased the rate of exhaustion of scarce natural resources, and brought the country close to a long-term crisis when the resources ran out.

In the real world, however, few if any people fit the description 'average'. Instead, most people are relatively poor and fall below the average, and a few people are well-off and stand far above the average. In South America some people are very rich and have hundreds of times the income and wealth of most poor people. In these circumstances, the income and wealth resulting from economic growth may be spread very unevenly among the population. The relatively few above-average people may take most of the gains and the many below-average people may gain very little or actually become worse off. It is therefore possible that while the economy grows, most people (the poor) may actually become poorer, while only a minority (the well off) become wealthier. Thus, growth does not necessarily benefit the whole population, or even the majority of the population. However, growth does at least always benefit a minority of the population.

The introduction of new high-technology industries, using foreign equipment and methods, may increase the total volume and value of production in a country. There are larger imports of equipment and raw materials and larger exports of finished products. This economic growth is likely to enrich a number of foreign companies, local investors and merchants dealing with imports and exports. It may also benefit the emerging middle class of technicians and skilled industrial workers. In many cases, however, such new, high-technology industries manufacture goods which are slightly cheaper than those that are hand-made, or produced in small workshops. As a result, many traditional producers lose their jobs and become far poorer. For example, new plastics and metal-working factories using a lot of complex machinery and relatively little labour begin to sell cheap, hard-wearing plastic and metal containers. These new products replace the old-fashioned pottery containers. A few hundred new jobs may be created in the new factories and in some new shops, but thousands of jobs may be lost for the

Fig. 1.3 Traditional pottery and hand-woven rope on sale in the village market of Chugchilan in the Andes of Ecuador.

traditional pottery workers, transporters and traders (Fig. 1.3).

Economic growth may not only affect inequalities between different social groups, but also between the regions of a country and between different countries. If growth is greatest in the poorest areas, spatial inequalities are likely to fall. If it is greatest in the richest areas, spatial inequalities are likely to increase. In South America there is no consistent pattern of change in the inequalities between countries, as many of the countries have undergone marked and contrasting fluctuations in economic growth rates since 1960. Within most of the South American countries, however, the economic growth of a core or central area often outstrips the growth of the surrounding periphery.

The effects of economic growth can only be judged by studying their impact on different areas as well as on different social groups. We then find out whether the particular growth taking place is actually increasing or decreasing inequalities. We also discover whether the new wealth of some groups or areas is linked with other groups or areas getting poorer. Once this is studied, and we have assessed how rapidly the natural resources are being used up, we can then make a general value judgment as to whether the benefits of growth outweigh the costs. In other words we are in a position to judge whether the specific type of growth taking place is desirable.

Some experts argue that almost all economic growth is good. They feel that increasing inequalities, some social groups becoming poorer, and the depletion of various natural resources should all be ignored. They see economic growth as progress, stimulating people to adapt to the changing circumstances and to overcome problems of poverty and resource use. In other words, to them, growth and development are the same. In contrast, other experts argue that most forms of economic growth are bad, precisely because they increase inequalities, make certain social groups poorer and use up key natural resources. Since they see such growth as bad, they would not choose to call it development. They prefer to use the term 'development' only for the more balanced forms of growth which are genuinely beneficial to most of the population. It is in this latter sense

11

that we separate the terms growth and development in this book. We talk of 'growth' when we refer to economic growth, without implying that it is desirable or undesirable. In contrast, we only talk of 'development' when we are making a positive value judgment ourselves, or when we are describing the views of a particular interest group.

Development as modernization

When development is associated with growth, it is viewed in economic terms of production and consumption. This is a very materialistic approach and suggests that making progress and getting richer are one and the same thing. However there is an alternative, less economic, approach which emphasizes the social and cultural aspects of development. This involves recognizing a particular type of society and economy in the world as the most advanced and modern, and seeing all the others as relatively backward and traditional in comparison. The most advanced and modern parts of the world are seen as spreading ideas and technology which 'improve' the rest of the world. All countries can be ranked according to how similar they are to the most advanced countries, or in other words according to their degree of 'modernization'. Countries are thought to develop by modernizing and becoming more similar to the most advanced country. The most underdeveloped countries are those which are the most traditional, and therefore the least modernized. The whole approach is usually known as modernization theory. It has been used most often in the United States as a means of interpreting the patterns and processes of change occurring around the world. It is normally assumed there that the United States is the most modern country, and that modern ideas and technology spread from the United States to the rest of the world.

Most people object to modernization theory because it reflects the views of a single cultural group. The theory only takes the viewpoint of one group, which considers its own ideas and technology superior to those of all other groups. Some people also object to modernization theory because it gives 'advanced' countries, like the United States, an excuse to further their own interests by preaching their superiority and selling their own products in the poor countries. Those who oppose the theory also point out that some countries, particularly Japan, have achieved rapid economic growth without copying all the western cultural values. If all countries did modernize by following the example of the United States or the countries of north-west Europe, the result would be a world with very little diversity and probably with less capacity for innovation.

Development as increasing welfare and quality of life

Dissatisfaction with the ideas of development as growth and development as modernization has led to the concept of development as increasing welfare and the quality of life. In this way non-economic factors are taken into account as well as the simple increase of material wealth, and most problems of modernization theory are avoided. 'Welfare' and 'the quality of life' are two different ways of expressing general well-being, going beyond simple economic factors to include a variety of social, cultural and environmental factors as well. It is believed that people seek broad satisfaction and happiness, rather than just more money and more goods. Satisfaction and happiness depend on such factors as health, entertainment, working conditions, political freedom, and social relationships. It is generally assumed that satisfaction and happiness are very difficult to measure and to compare between different time periods and countries. However, it is possible to use a variety of social indicators. These social indicators include measures of life expectancy (the average length of life), infant mortality (the death rate of babies), rates of crime and delinquency, participation in politics and community affairs, unemployment and environmental pollution. Various specialists have suggested ways in which these indicators can be grouped together with economic statistics and made into a general index of welfare or the quality of life. Such an index would provide a broad measure of development. As yet there is no agreement on what data should be included in determining these measures or on how the different statistics could be put together.

There will never be complete agreement on a single index of welfare or of the quality of life, as the whole idea of choosing and measuring the factors to take into account, depends on political, moral and even religious judgments. Instead, people tend to refer to individual social indicators, without combining them into any single index. Thus, for example, the discussions of the changes which occurred in Brazil between 1965 and 1975 tend to contrast the rapid rates of economic growth with the very slow progress in improving education provision, reducing malnutrition, or increasing life expectancy. Such an approach suggests that rapid economic development took place, but that no corresponding process of social development occurred. Those who favour growth at virtually any cost will praise the Brazilian development process. In contrast, those who stress the importance of welfare and quality of life will argue that economic growth has received too much attention and investment in Brazil, and that social concerns have been neglected. This argument is reinforced by a simple comparison with Chile, which has experienced lower economic growth rates than Brazil over most of the last three decades, but which has made more substantial progress in improving social provision (Table 1.1).

Alternative ways of defining underdevelopment

The simplest definition of underdevelopment stems directly from the idea of development as economic growth. Underdevelopment is seen as extreme poverty and the almost total absence of growth. The poorest countries are therefore the most underdeveloped, and within individual countries the poorest regions are the most underdeveloped.

Many people feel that economic growth should only be described as development if the majority of the population gradually becomes better off. They tend to associate underdevelopment with high levels of inequality between rich and poor, as well as with absolute poverty. In their view, even if there is no overall growth in GNP, reducing inequalities is a form of development as there is a desirable redistribution of income and wealth from rich to poor. In the same way, when inequalities increase they see underdevelopment as increasing, even if there is significant economic growth.

Table 1.1   Four indicators of change in Brazil and Chile 1960–1985

Years	Average annual % rates of growth in GDP	Average life expectancy at birth in years	Year	% literacy (popn aged over 14)	% in secondary education[a]
BRAZIL					
1960–65	4.5	55.9	1960	60.3	11
1965–70	7.7	57.9	1965	66.2	27
1970–75	10.8	59.8	1970	68.7	32
1975–80	6.8	61.8	1974	–	35
1980–85	2.7	63.4			
CHILE					
1960–65	5.0	58.0	1960	83.6	24
1965–70	3.9	60.6	1970	89.0	39
1970–75	−0.6	63.8	1980	91.6	55
1975–80	7.5	67.6	1984	–	66
1980–85	1.2	69.7			

[a.] Population attending secondary school establishments as a percentage of the population aged 14 to 19.

Sources: Inter-American Development Bank, *1987 Report*; United Nations, *Statistical Yearbook for Latin America 1985*; World Bank, *World Development Report 1983, 1987*.

The idea of development as modernization produces a corresponding idea of underdevelopment as backwardness or traditionalism. Those countries and areas which are least similar to the advanced, modern countries are viewed as backward or underdeveloped. Those countries which are modifying to absorb the new ideas, values and technologies, are described as developing or modernizing. Such a view of underdevelopment contains all the culture-bound thinking of modernization theory. It implies that the more developed countries are superior to the less developed.

A final and very different view of underdevelopment stems from the concept of self-reliance. In this view, countries which are simply poor and isolated are 'undeveloped' rather than 'underdeveloped'. Development consists of their inhabitants overcoming poverty and isolation through their own efforts and decisions, without being conquered by other countries or becoming too reliant on outside help and investment. Where the government of a country has control over its own affairs and is able to act freely and independently of other countries, there is scope for self-reliance. This means that the country finds its own solutions to its own problems and uses local resources and technology as much as possible.

The view of underdevelopment as resulting from the loss of national self-reliance may be better understood if we consider the case of an imaginary undeveloped country which somehow avoided becoming a European colony. In this country the government and powerful interest groups manage to maintain self-reliance while bringing about major economic growth, avoiding widening social and economic inequalities, and improving the quality of life for most people. Under such circumstances, the country would be developing without ever being underdeveloped. Indeed, if the country continued this development process for many years, it would generally be considered to have entered the ranks of the world's more developed nations.

The above example of a fictitious country is intended to show how idealistic the idea of development through self-reliance really is. Self-reliance may well be an ideal for governments to aim at, but there are many reasons why few poor countries have achieved it to any significant degree in the last half century. Only a handful of countries outside Europe have managed to avoid a period of European colonial rule in which self-reliance was deliberately suppressed by the colonial power. Even if such colonial rule was avoided, or if there was a deliberate attempt to restore self-reliance after independence from colonial rule, governments often prove weak, and there is threat or intervention from powerful foreign countries, foreign companies and banks. In such circumstances, those governments do not have full control over their countries' affairs and the future of their countries is determined more by external factors than by internal ones.

When a country is poor, when its government has relatively little control over national affairs, and when the real power to decide on the nation's future lies with richer and more technologically-advanced countries, self-reliance can be little more than a dream. When this combination of problems occurs, as it does in most Latin American, African and Asian countries, some specialists choose to describe the countries as 'dependent', that is dependent on outside decisions, resources, investments and technologies to such an extent that their governments are incapable of effective independent action. As dependency on outside circumstances and pressures increases, the country is seen as becoming more and more underdeveloped in relation to the richer countries on which it depends. Underdevelopment is therefore viewed as a result of the way in which the country has been incorporated into the world economic and political system. This contrasts strongly with modernization theory, which sees underdevelopment as natural backwardness. For those who admire national self-reliance, increasing underdevelopment is associated with increasing dependency, and with types of economic growth which lead to growing inequalities between rich and poor.

To summarize, the different interpretations of the term 'underdevelopment' divide into two major schools of thought, 'the enlightenment school' and 'the dependence–dominance school'. Those who favour the enlightenment view see the whole world as originally having been underdeveloped, and then certain countries developing more complex civilizations, systems of government and technologies. These countries are described as the most developed and they are seen as having a favourable influence on the remaining countries. The remaining countries are still underdeveloped or less developed, but they are gradually progressing within a world economic system which helps both rich and poor countries. In contrast to such a view, those who belong to the dependence–dominance school see the whole world as originally having been undeveloped, with a few countries then expanding their areas of influence to control the interests of other countries. Such control may occur directly through conquest and colonial rule, as in the case of the Spanish, Portuguese, British and French empires. Alternatively, it may be exercised indirectly through the major banks, trading companies and investors, as in the case of the most recent involvement of the United States, West Germany and Japan in the affairs of African, Asian and

Latin American countries. Direct control is normally referred to as colonialism or imperialism, while indirect control is often called neo-colonialism or external domination. In the dependence–dominance view, dominant countries develop and become richer at the expense of other countries. Those other countries, through loss of control over their own affairs, become increasingly dependent on the dominant countries. In effect, the dependent countries, most of which are located in Africa, Asia and Latin America, become increasingly underdeveloped as they lose their self-reliance. They are incorporated on unfavourable terms into a world economic system which is largely organized for the benefit of the richer dominant countries, particularly those of North America, Western Europe, and Japan.

Development and underdevelopment: nice terms to hide unpleasant facts

The twentieth century has seen the foundation and growth of international organizations such as the United Nations and the World Bank. These organizations have been concerned with development issues and with the inequalities between rich and poor countries. Discussion on such issues has been encouraged by the governments of many poor and often newly-independent countries, by charitable groups in the rich countries, and by commercial interests keen to increase international trade. There has been a marked growth, in terms of both quantity and quality, of international statistics on levels of economic and social progress in different countries, so that we are able to map and analyse the patterns on a world scale (Figs. 1.4 and 1.5). This has led, in turn, to the emergence of a whole new academic subject for the study of such information, and for the discussion of alternative policies to improve economic and social conditions. This subject is generally known as 'Development Studies', and can be broadly defined as: 'the critical examination of alternative processes of social and economic change and of policies designed to encourage such change'.

With the emergence of Development Studies and the growing discussion in international organizations on the relations between rich and poor countries, there have been many changes in the use of terms. When the poorest countries were European colonies, the Europeans tended to refer to themselves as coming from 'civilized' or 'advanced' countries, and to refer to all other parts of the world as 'primitive' or 'backward'. As the former colonies became independent, the terms were gradually changed to give a more favourable impression of the poorer countries. Thus, the former 'civilized' or 'advanced' countries were usually retitled 'developed' or 'more developed' countries, and the former 'primitive' or 'backward' countries became 'underdeveloped' or 'less developed'. Many people, however, still felt that such names did not show sufficient respect for the poorer countries, and so new terms were invented: 'newly-emergent nations', 'developing countries', 'Third World countries', and most recently of all, 'the South'. Each of these terms was intended to describe the countries of Latin America, Africa, the Middle East, South and South-East Asia, the Caribbean and the Pacific, distinguishing this whole group from the countries of North America and Europe, the USSR, Japan, Australia and New Zealand. In effect, the whole world was

*The 'First World' is usually considered to consist of North America, Western Europe, Japan, Australia and New Zealand (the group which are often called 'advanced capitalist countries'). The 'Second World' is usually considered to consist of the USSR, the Soviet Block communist countries of Eastern Europe (Poland, East Germany, Czechoslovakia, Hungary, Roumania and Bulgaria), Yugoslavia, Albania and Mongolia.

divided into two major blocks of countries, more-or-less corresponding to the dependent–dominant split. This division was seen to represent differences in terms of recent historical experience (the colonized and the colonizers) and in terms of current political and economic interests on the world scene (the 'have-nots' or 'South', and the 'haves' or 'North').

Any division of the world into two groups of countries, such as the division between developing and developed countries, or between the Third World and the First and Second Worlds* (Fig. 1.4), is open to discussion. There are similarities between countries placed in the same group, but there are also enormous differences. The groups are labelled as much for international political reasons, as because they have any real common characteristics. The terms 'developing countries' and 'Third World' are intended to define, and actually help to establish, a set of common interests. They create a basis for a political alliance of Latin American, African and Asian governments to press the richer countries of the Northern Hemisphere for what the Third World countries see as fairer prices in international trade. The Third World governments press for higher and more stable prices for tropical products, more fully reflecting the massive amounts of labour that go into their production, and lower prices for North American, European and Japanese imports. They also seek cheaper loans, the reduction of their debts, the provision of more economic aid to poor countries, and better access to technological information.

For the purposes of this book, it is particularly important to note the special characteristics of South America. It is a major world region which is generally viewed as part of the Third World or the 'developing countries'. However, in many respects it is no more similar to Africa and Asia than it is to North America and Western Europe (Table 1.2). In terms of international trade and investment, the South American countries are closely linked to North America, Western Europe and Japan, with only very limited connections to the Soviet Block, Africa, Asia (apart from Japan) and Australia. The main cultural and religious ties are with southern Europe, and to a lesser but growing extent with North America and north-west Europe. Almost the only countries in the world with similar political history are those of Central America. Most of South America was colonized by European countries long before the conquest of substantial parts of Africa and Asia, and independence was anything from 50 to 150 years before that of most African countries. Indeed, almost all of South America was independent before countries like Kenya and Zambia even became European colonies.

In terms of GDP per capita, the South American countries are generally much poorer than most West European or North American countries, but much better off than most African or Asian countries. South American countries have great internal inequalities and widespread poverty, but they do not have the desperate poverty which exists in most of tropical Africa and South Asia. While there may be interesting comparisons with African and Asian countries, because of their colonial background and their present-day dependence upon the world's richer countries, there are very good reasons for studying South America as a

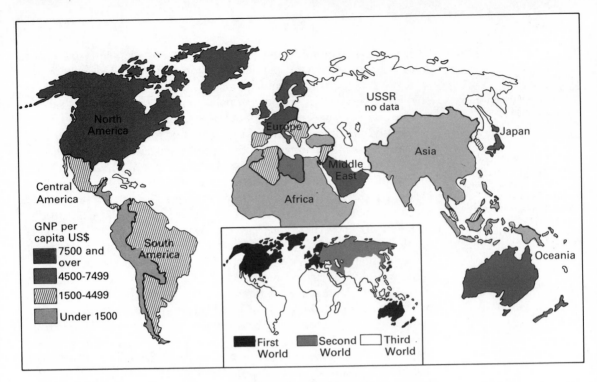

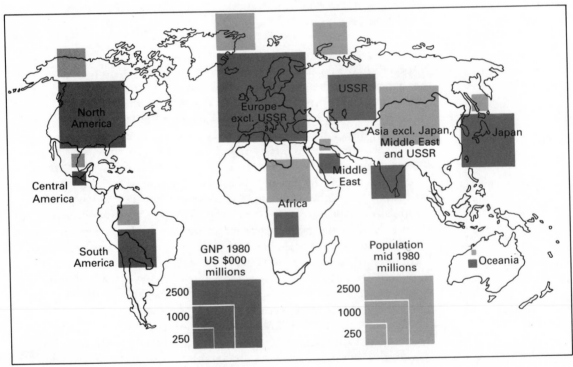

Fig. 1.4 GNP per capita 1985. Owing to the small scale of the map, small countries are classified the same as their larger neighbours. Source: World Bank, *World Development Report 1987*.

Fig. 1.5 Total GNP in relation to total population by major world regions 1980. Data for Kampuchea, Iran, Laos, Lebanon and Vietnam have been excluded. Source: World Bank, *World Bank Atlas 1981 and 1983*.

Table 1.2 Basic indicators of development: South America and selected countries in other continents

Country	GNP per capita		Urban[a] pop. as % of total pop. 1985	Daily calorie supply per capita 1985	Life expectancy at birth (years) 1985	Infant mortality rate per thousand 1985	Adult literacy rate (%) 1980
	US $ 1985	Average annual growth % 1965–85					
SOUTH AMERICA							
Argentina	2,130	0.2	84	3,221	70	34	93
Bolivia	470	−0.2	44	2,146	53	117	63
Brazil	1,640	4.3	73	2,633	65	67	76
Chile	1,430	−0.2	83	2,602	70	22	88[b]
Colombia	1,320	2.9	67	2,574	65	48	81
Ecuador	1,160	3.5	52	2,054	66	67	81
Guyana	500	−0.2	31	—	65	45[c]	91
Paraguay	860	3.9	41	2,796	66	43	84
Peru	1,010	0.2	68	2,171	59	94	80
Suriname	2,580	3.4	58	—	66	28[c]	80
Uruguay	1,650	1.4	85	2,695	72	29	94
Venezuela	3,080	0.5	85	2,583	70	37	82
AFRICA							
Ethiopia	110	0.2	15	1,681	45	168	15
Tanzania	290	—	14	2,335	52	110	79
ASIA							
Bangladesh	150	0.4	18	1,899	51	123	26
India	270	1.7	25	2,189	56	89	36
EUROPE							
France	9,540	2.8	73	3,359	78	8	99
UK	8,460	1.6	92	3,131	75	9	99
NORTH AMERICA							
Canada	13,680	2.4	77	3,432	76	8	99
USA	16,690	1.7	74	3,663	76	11	99

[a.] Using national definitions of urban, which will vary between countries.
[b.] Data for 1975.
[c.] Data for 1984.
Sources: United Nations, *Demographic Yearbook 1978, Statistical Yearbook for Latin America, 1985;* World Bank, *World Development Report 1983, 1987.*

unique world region. Some people may wish to link South America to Africa and Asia as part of the Third World. Others may wish to link it to Central and North America, Western Europe, Australia and New Zealand as part of the 'Western World'. Both such groupings, however, should be based upon a firm understanding of the characteristics of particular world regions like South America, and of the countries that make up those regions. It is to the task of establishing a broad description and understanding of South America that we turn our attention in the following chapters.

2 The legacy of colonialism and incorporation into the world economy

Pre-conquest and conquest

Many of the distinctive socio-economic characteristics of present-day South America have their roots deep in the past, some owing their origins to the societies which existed on the continent before European discovery. Prior to Christopher Columbus's famous voyage of discovery to the Caribbean in 1492, there had been no historically well-recorded European contact with any part of the Americas. His voyage signalled the start of the Spanish and Portuguese conquest of South America and the introduction of new cultures.

White people from Europe entered a continent occupied by American Indians. The native animals and plants of the continent had developed in isolation from Europe, Africa and Asia for many thousands of years. For food crops the Indian populations relied chiefly on maize, manioc, quinoa, beans and potatoes, and their only large domesticated animals were llamas and alpacas. In the highland belt of the Andes and along the Pacific coast of Peru, a number of advanced Indian civilizations had developed. Although none created writing, or knew of wheeled transport, they had an advanced agriculture and considerable knowledge of irrigation and terracing (Fig. 2.1). By the early sixteenth century much of the Andean Indian population had been incorporated into the Inca Empire, which stretched from northern Ecuador, south to Talca in Chile. Most Indians lived in scattered villages with their houses dispersed amongst the fields. However, in parts of the Inca Empire there were major urban centres. Cuzco, in the Andes of southern Peru, was probably the largest city, and the unique Inca building styles are still evident in the urban fabric today. Towns also existed in the Chibcha kingdoms which occupied parts of the Andes in present-day Colombia. The vast tropical forest lands of the Amazon and Orinoco basins and the northern and northwestern coastlands of South America, were entirely different in their human geography from the Andes. They were much more sparsely populated by Indian tribes which lived by hunting and gathering and the limited cultivation of crops. Most of the southern and eastern areas of South America, stretching from present-day North-East Brazil to Tierra del Fuego, were only very sparsely populated by such tribes. There were, however, some more significant Indian population concentrations in present-day eastern Paraguay (the Guarani), and in southern Chile (the Mapuche).

The new lands were divided between Portugal and Spain by the Treaty of Tordesillas of 1494. This laid down a dividing line from the North Pole to the South Pole, which ran 370 leagues west of the Cape Verde Islands, (between 48° and 49° west of Greenwich). Land west of that line was to belong to Spain and land to the east was to belong to Portugal. Thus, before the continent of South America had even been discovered,

Fig. 2.1 Pre-conquest agricultural terraces in the Urubamba valley near the village of Pisac in the Andes of south Peru.

Portugal had been allocated the eastern portion, establishing a basis for the present-day contrast between the Portuguese-speaking population of Brazil and the Spanish-speaking populations of other South American countries.

The Spaniards approached their new territories from early bases in the Caribbean and concentrated first on establishing colonies in Mexico and Central America. The famous conquistador, Pizarro, led seaborne expeditions south from Panama to the coastlands of Colombia, Ecuador and Peru in the 1520s. In 1532 he landed in northern Peru with a small army of Spaniards, and after a tip-off from native informants, he approached the town of Cajamarca where he was able to capture the Inca, the supreme ruler of the Inca Empire. After the Inca's execution in 1533, the vast empire was rapidly taken over. Other expeditions in the 1530s, with different leaders, established the Spaniards in Bolivia,

Argentina and Chile to the south, and in Colombia and Venezuela to the north.

The Spanish conquest of South America was a massive sweep of the western side of the continent and a far grander affair than the small-scale efforts of the Portuguese in Brazil during the early sixteenth century. Cabral discovered the northeastern coast of Brazil in 1500 and formally took possession of the territory for the King of Portugal. Portugal, however, was already committed to colonies in Africa and Asia, and as her rulers were more interested in commerce than in colonization, only a few small trading settlements were established in Brazil by 1530. Colonization was later encouraged by the Portuguese monarchy, however, to ensure that the new lands were not taken over by other countries.

The conquest of South America brought about huge changes in the continent's human geography, completely altering its development patterns and trends. New cultures were introduced by the Spanish and Portuguese: new religion, languages, institutions and social organizations. The arrival of the Europeans brought about major changes in population, in the distribution and functions of towns, and in the economy. These topics will be considered under separate headings.

Population changes

The arrival of Europeans in the sixteenth century meant the introduction of new diseases which had devastating effects on the native Indian population. Measles, smallpox and influenza killed millions of Indians. Evidence for the pre-conquest period is limited, but in the former Inca Empire, covering the central Andes of South America, there may have been nine to twelve million people. By the 1570s the Indian population had probably fallen to about 1.5 million. In the other regions of South America, where the Indian population was generally much more sparsely distributed, the native population fell equally dramatically and whole tribes disappeared altogether.

The newly-arrived Europeans were generally of the 'white' Caucasian racial group, and most of them took Indian wives or concubines, so that their children were of mixed descent, becoming known as mestizos. A multi-racial and intermixed society was therefore created, with three fairly distinct groups. The whites formed the most powerful and wealthy group of the population and the Indians formed the poor and exploited mass. In an intermediate position were the mestizos, who normally adopted European dress and customs but were not usually admitted to the company and privileges of the select white group.

Soon after the conquest another race was introduced: the African Negro. Blacks were imported as slaves, particularly to North-East Brazil and to areas bordering the Caribbean. In these places unions between white men and black women produced mulatto children. Some racial mixing between Indians and blacks also occurred. Thus the foundations for the racial variety, and the uneven distribution of Indians, whites and blacks across South America, had already been laid by the close of the sixteenth century.

Colonial urban development

Most of the main cities in South America today were founded by the Spanish and Portuguese in the sixteenth century. An examination of the functions, location and planning of the early settlements helps us to understand the present-day pattern.

The Spaniards and the Portuguese differed considerably in the role they gave to town foundation, with the result that early differences arose between the settlement geography of Spanish America and Brazil. Spain had a far stronger urban tradition than Portugal, where agriculture and fishing were more central to the society. These differences became more pronounced in South America because Spain was allocated those lands which already possessed Indian urban civilizations. The Spanish conquerors used towns as instruments of colonization, treating them as bases for the exploration and administration of the surrounding territories. In Brazil there were no pre-conquest urban settlements, and in the sixteenth century the Portuguese invested relatively little in the settlement of their new American territories. The resulting distribution of towns in Brazil was limited to a string of small port settlements along the coast, and towns were much less common and less impressive than in most of Spanish America.

Whether of Spanish or Portuguese foundation, the early towns and cities tended to have at least one of three basic functions: administration, trade or mining. Most urban centres were founded mainly for administrative reasons. At the local level, small towns were the centres for organizing tax collection and labour services from the Indian population, and for the introduction of Christianity. These towns were particularly concentrated in areas with a fairly dense Indian population, most notably in the Andean highlands of present-day Peru, Bolivia, Ecuador and Colombia. At the regional level, major administrative centres were established, often incorporating an Indian town, as was the case at Cajamarca, Huancayo and Cuzco in Peru. These regional administrative centres are generally still the chief provincial towns today. At the highest level were the cities founded to administer the huge territorial divisions later to become separate countries. In the Spanish Empire for example, Quito, founded in 1534, was created the capital of an Audiencia, or large administrative area, in 1563 and it is now the capital of Ecuador. Similarly, Lima was established as the capital of a Viceroyalty in 1535, and grew rapidly to a population of over 14,000 inhabitants by 1599. Today Lima remains the largest city in the Andean countries, and the capital of Peru.

Unlike the economy before conquest, which was mainly oriented to local and inter-regional trade, the economy of colonial South America was oriented towards seaborne trade with Europe. Many trading and port-towns were founded by the Spanish and Portuguese, and their functions often included the administration of large inland areas. In the sixteenth century, for example, the Spaniards established major port settlements at Panama, Guayaquil, Callao (the outport of Lima) and Valparaíso on the Pacific, and the Portuguese established such ports as Recife, Salvador and Rio de Janeiro on the Atlantic. The main factors in port location were the physical conditions of the harbour and the economic significance of the hinterland for trade with Europe. It was rare, therefore, for the new port-towns to be located on the sites of previous Indian settlements.

While administrative and port functions accounted for most of the sixteenth-century towns and cities, the discovery of rich mineral deposits in various parts of the continent led to the foundation of mining towns. Many of the mining towns were in remote and inaccessible areas; there was a particular concentration in the Andean mountains, and later also in the plateaus of East-Central Brazil. The earliest and most famous mining town was Potosí in Bolivia, where silver was discovered in 1545. The rich mines sparked off the spectacular growth of the city, which by 1573 was estimated to have 120,000 inhabitants, and by 1611 perhaps 160,000 inhabitants. Other mining settlements grew up around Potosí, and the linked, but distant, mining town of Huancavelica in central Peru grew rapidly after mercury was discovered there in 1563. Major mining activity did not appear in Brazil until the early eighteenth century, after gold was discovered in several parts of Minas Gerais. Various mining towns, including the famous and prosperous Ouro Preto, were founded in the Brazilian interior after these discoveries, representing the first phase of urban expansion away from the Atlantic coastal strip.

Most of the towns founded by the Spanish and many of those founded by the Portuguese were laid out according to a grid plan, with straight streets crossing one another at right angles. The main administrative and religious buildings were constructed around the central square, together with the houses of the most important colonists (Fig. 2.2). The square usually became the site for a weekly market and, as the town expanded, more and more shops and warehouses were established close to the centre. Gradually, therefore, the towns tended to diversify their functions, assuming more of a commercial role and functioning as service centres for their surrounding rural areas. In most of the towns, however, there were also important agricultural functions. Some small-scale farmers lived in each town and farmed holdings around the edge of the urban area, and most of the rich townsfolk living around the central square owned large estates in the surrounding region. The poorest townsfolk were generally mestizos, Indians, or black slaves, and they worked as casual labourers, porters, petty traders and servants. Most of them lived in one-room huts towards the edge of the town, but some of the servants lived in the relatively elegant houses of their masters around the town centre.

Though the Spaniards and Portuguese founded towns in remote inland areas of South America where there were major concentrations of Indian population or large mineral reserves, most of their towns were founded on, or close to, the coast. The sea offered communication links with the mother countries of Spain and Portugal, and travel by sea was generally easier, more comfortable and cheaper than overland travel. Even today, though there are many inland towns and cities in the Andes, the majority of South America's urban centres are located in coastal lowland areas of the continent. With good reason, some geographers and politicians even refer to South America as 'the hollow continent'. This name reflects the tradition of Spanish and Portuguese settlement close to the coast and the relative lack of settlement in the vast central area of South America, and particularly in the sparsely-populated Amazon basin.

A further legacy from the past is the lack of a closely interrelated urban system. In the colonial era, because administration and trade were

Fig. 2.2 The Plaza de la Independencia in Quito, the capital of Ecuador. This is one of the city's main squares, and is surrounded by colonial buildings.

organized from Spain and Portugal, each of the major South American cities interacted chiefly with the European countries, and not with other cities and towns in the colonies. The main urban centres in South America were largely independent of each other. The strength of the links between a few cities and the mother country is probably reflected today in the particularly large size of those cities (e.g. Lima and Buenos Aires) relative to the other urban centres in their countries, which seem small and provincial in comparison.

Although the legacy of the early colonial urban foundations in the present-day distribution of urban centres is extremely strong, the exact sites of today's towns and cities are often not inherited from the sixteenth century. The early settlements were small and provisional, and not all the chosen sites were successful. Sometimes a severe earthquake or volcanic eruption caused a change of site. The west coast and the Andes, after all, lie on the active circum-Pacific arc of tectonic activity. Usually, however, the site changes involved a move of only a few kilometres.

The colonial extractive economy

Most of the Spaniards and Portuguese who travelled to South America in the sixteenth century went in search of wealth, choosing those activities which they thought would yield the greatest financial return. Conquest and colonization were accompanied by exploitation of the continent's physical resources and its population. Economic activity after the conquest was mainly focused on the mine or the large landed estate. The operation of each depended on a labour supply. Given the small numbers of Europeans and the fact that most of them despised manual labour, the continent's mining and farming activities relied on a native labour force and, where this was absent, on imported labour, the African slave. The exploitation and degradation of the Indian and black labour force is often viewed as the chief social legacy of the colonial economy to modern South America. Although the colonial system of labour organization is now dead, the racist and elitist attitudes that it bred still remain today. Other more obvious legacies of the colonial economy are seen in the settlement pattern and the landholding structure.

Mining

Mining played a key role in the colonial economic growth of South America. The reserves of gold, silver and other precious metals attracted settlers to the new territories. They provided the essential finance for the administration of the colonies, and large quantities of wealth were shipped to enrich the royal families and other elites of Spain and Portugal. The mines stimulated the growth of towns and had an impact on large areas of the continent. The silver mines around Potosí, for example, relied on Indian workers drafted in from long distances. Thousands of mules were reared for use in transport, and the early colonial economy of much of present-day Bolivia and Peru was dominated by mining.

The large landed estate

The evolution of the large landed estate as a feature of the colonial economy has had a lasting impact on the rural geography of South America. Many of the present-day problems arising from the uneven distribution of landholdings owe their origins to the colonial era. The early settlers from Spain and Portugal wanted to acquire land on the continent. Landownership gave them status and a considerable amount of control over the labour of the people living on their land, as well as the chance to make money from agriculture or ranching. The large landed estates could be divided into two groups, just as they can today: the 'haciendas' and the 'plantations'. The operation of both categories was very different from traditional Indian farming, which involved a mixture of communally held land and individual smallholdings, and the cultivation of a wide variety of crops.

The hacienda was a large estate producing a range of crops and raising cattle. Some of the products were for subsistence, in other words they were consumed on the hacienda itself. The remainder of the products were to supply local and regional demands, particularly from the townsfolk. Most haciendas were built up in the sixteenth and seventeenth centuries by gradually taking over the land of Indian communities. Sometimes the Indians were dispossessed by crown grants which gave their land and the right to control their labour to a leading Spanish or Portuguese settler. In other cases the Indians actually sold their land, but more often it was simply taken over when they died in the epidemics or forced labour in the mines which followed the conquest. Many of the colonial haciendas have survived until the twentieth century. A study of the Chancay Valley in Peru, for example, has shown that in 1964, 18 haciendas controlled 80 per cent of the whole cultivated area, and that 14 of these haciendas had been established by the end of the sixteenth century.

The plantation was a large estate specializing in one or two crops for export. It used a more tightly disciplined system of production than the hacienda, generally operating largely independently of the surrounding areas and forming an 'enclave' economy. The plantations were generally managed by Europeans, used European technology, and were mainly worked by a slave labour force originally brought from Africa. Most of the plantations established in the first century of Spanish and Portuguese colonial rule were located in North-East Brazil and specialized in the production of sugar, molasses and rum for export to Europe. The soil and climatic conditions were well suited to sugar-cane and there were many sheltered harbours along the coast for the establishment of port-towns like Natal, Recife and Salvador. The only early difficulty was the lack of an abundant Indian labour force. This problem was solved, at the cost of great human suffering, by the import of about 50,000 black slaves in the sixteenth century and over 500,000 in the seventeenth century.

The plantation was not a major feature of the Spanish colonies in South America until after independence in the nineteenth century. During the colonial period, however, there were some sugar and cotton plantations in coastal Peru, and, particularly in the late eighteenth century various cacao plantations were established in the Guayas basin in the coastal lowlands of present-day Ecuador.

Independence: foreign penetration and primary exports

For almost the whole of South America, the colonial era came to an end in the early nineteenth century. Over a period of 15 years, the Spanish and Portuguese colonies fought for their independence. The final major battle was in 1824 when Spain lost control of its last territories in South America. Portuguese power in the continent ended in 1822 when Brazil declared itself an independent empire with its own Emperor, Pedro I, the son of the Portuguese King. The newly independent countries, which were all republics except Brazil, were based on the old colonial administrative regions (Fig. 2.3). After some subdivision during the 1820s, the South American countries acquired their present-day names and most of their boundaries (Fig. 2.4). Brazil finally became a republic in 1889, when the Emperor Pedro II agreed to abdicate. The only remnants of colonial rule

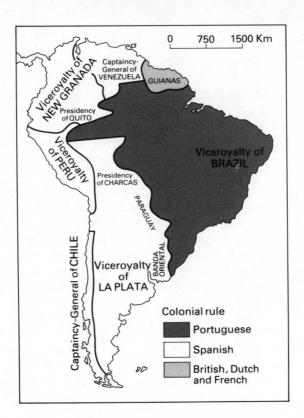

Fig. 2.3 The principal administrative divisions of South America in 1800.

left in the continent were then the Guianas, where the British, the Dutch, and the French retained separate colonies, and the Falkland Islands, a remote British outpost in the South Atlantic, claimed by Argentina. British Guiana finally gained independence as Guyana in 1966, and Dutch Guiana, called Suriname, became fully independent in 1975. French Guiana became an overseas department of France in 1946. Today this leaves only the Falkland Islands, Islas Malvinas, under colonial rule, and they have only about 2,000 inhabitants.

Independence marked the legal ending of the colonial economic system which had reflected the concern of Spain and Portugal to maintain economies which were profitable to them, the mother countries. Their emphasis on mining and the production of plantation crops had been accompanied by a policy of discouraging manufacturing industry in the colonies. In all populated areas of the continent, colonial rule had created a group of landowners resident in the towns, with a comfortable life style in great contrast to the poverty of the Indians, mestizos and blacks. The colonial system had created major differences in wealth and social status between these different sectors of the population. It also left an economic legacy which was slow to disappear.

Although independence marked the ending of colonial restrictions and opened the way for the formation of new trading links, there was little economic change in South America before the 1850s. The colonial pattern tended to continue, and even slavery lingered on in some parts of the continent until it was finally abolished at the end of the nineteenth century. Brazil continued to have an export-oriented agricultural economy based on plantations of sugar, and later also of cotton. In Spanish America, mining was still vital to the economies of Peru, Bolivia

Fig. 2.4 International frontiers in South America, and the major regional divisions of Brazil.

and Chile. Outside Brazil where there was political stability, economic growth was held back by political troubles, including some civil wars, frequent armed conflicts, and many changes of government. Moreover, most countries, including Brazil, were at war over boundary disputes during several of the decades following independence. The worst affected was undoubtedly Paraguay, which fought and lost the War of the Triple Alliance against Brazil, Argentina and Uruguay between 1865 and 1870. Paraguay's population was reduced by more than half, falling to less than a quarter of a million by the end of the war.

Greater involvement in the world economy

Despite the setbacks of the War of the Triple Alliance and various smaller-scale conflicts, the second half of the nineteenth century in most of South America was characterized by more stable political conditions than the first half. This relative stabilization was paralleled by fuller integration into the rapidly-expanding world economy. It was a period of fast-growing demand for raw materials from the expanding industries of north-west Europe and also from the newer industries of North America. In addition, there were strong pressures from European and North American industries to expand their markets around the world, and growth in trade was considerably helped by the new technologies of steamship and rail transport.

After 1850, therefore, several of the South American countries experienced periods of relatively rapid economic growth. Because the timing, nature and scale of this economic growth varied considerably from country to country and from region to region, this increased spatial inequalities within the continent. Many of these inequalities persist to the present day, particularly the relative prosperity of the southwestern third of South America (Argentina, Uruguay, Chile, South and South-East Brazil) compared with most of the rest of the continent (the Andean countries, Paraguay, and the Brazilian North-East and Amazonia). Economic growth was mainly associated with increased trade and investment, and with the growing penetration of South America by trading companies and investors from north-west Europe, and later also from North America. The expanding economies of South America were characterized by exports of primary products (goods extracted directly from the land and waters through mining, farming, forestry and fishing), and by imports of industrial products.

Ever since the late nineteenth century, there have been major differences of opinion about the increasing European and North American penetration of the South American economies. Those who favour free trade and foreign investment tend to see this penetration as highly beneficial, bringing economic growth and modernization to South America. In contrast, those who favour a more self-reliant model of national development argue that the nineteenth century saw nothing more than the replacement of Spanish and Portuguese colonialism with neo-colonial dependence on a new set of dominant countries. In the nineteenth century the most important dominant country as an investor and trading partner for the South American countries was Britain, but by the early twentieth century the United States was taking over the main dominant role.

In the second half of the nineteenth century, the pressure of industrial and population growth in Europe reached South America in three main ways. First, there was heavy demand for opportunities to emigrate from Europe, and particularly to countries with temperate climates similar to those of Europe. Most of the South American governments adopted policies favouring European immigration, and several million Europeans settled in South America, and especially in Argentina, South and South-East Brazil, Uruguay and Chile. Second, there was the search for new sources of food and raw materials, such as sugar, coffee, fertilizers, and metal ores. Third, there was a desire to find new outlets for European investment. These pressures occurred at a time of major advances in transport technology. Regular ocean and river steamship services became common in the second half of the nineteenth century after their gradual introduction in the 1820s. Refrigerated ships were introduced in the 1870s and the ocean transport of food products became easier. On land the first railways were completed in the 1850s but all were short and it was not until later in the century that good railway systems had been established in some regions, such as north-central Argentina, and South-East Brazil. Both the railway and the steamship made it possible to transport goods cheaply over long distances. Almost all developments were either foreign-owned or foreign-financed, particularly by the British, and were an important part of foreign penetration into the continent.

Primary exports: the economic and social impact

In order to illustrate the impact of the expansion of exports of primary products after 1850, we present three contrasting examples: Peru, which specialized in the export of minerals and tropical plantation crops; South-East Brazil, which specialized in coffee, a sub-tropical crop; and the Pampas of Argentina and Uruguay, which specialized in livestock and temperate-climate grains. These three examples are related to the possible ways in which a thriving export activity might encourage broad-based and long-term economic growth. In theory, at least, such growth might occur in three principal ways. First, by providing well-paid employment for a large sector of the population. This leads to increased consumer demand (because people have more money to spend), which in turn stimulates domestic trade and the production of a wide range of goods. The more people involved in the expanding export economy, the greater the beneficial effects are likely to be. Second, the particular export activity may involve the construction of new transport links and power supplies, and thus provide a basic infrastructure for other types of economic activity. Third, the revenues generated by the export activity can be invested in other sectors of the economy, for example, in roads or new industries. In addition to these three points, a thriving export activity can also contribute towards social change by lessening the power and influence of the small group, or elite, which had been traditionally important. This reduces one of the barriers to the achievement of greater social and economic equality amongst different sectors of the population.

Peru

In Peru, guano, sugar and metal ores were key exports in the nineteenth and early twentieth centuries. Guano, the accumulated droppings of millions of sea birds nesting on off-shore islands, became Peru's major export between the 1840s and 1880s. It was a superb fertilizer for use in European agriculture, and it was exported on a large scale. Sugar, which was mainly cultivated in the irrigated northern coastlands, became a boom crop for Peru in the 1860s and 1870s (Fig. 2.5). In the late nineteenth and early twentieth centuries it was Peru's principal export, and the former plantation owners were displaced by foreign businessmen who transformed sugar production with new equipment and organization. New foreign-owned companies organized the production and marketing of sugar in the same kind of way as the modern multinational companies (see Chapter 3). The demand for metals from the industrializing nations stimulated the opening of new mines in central Peru and the construction of the Central Railway from Callao to La Oroya by 1893; a foreign company built the railway, and the expanding mines were largely operated by foreigners. In this new mining era, silver and gold were replaced as the

Fig. 2.5 The Paramonga valley in the northern coastlands of Peru. Sugar-cane covers the irrigated valley floor. In the foreground are the mud walls of the Pativilca fortress, which dates from before the Spanish conquest.

most important metals by copper, and then from the 1920s by lead and zinc. In 1901 the American-controlled Cerro de Pasco Corporation was established and became the largest copper producer in Peru.

During the nineteenth and early twentieth centuries, therefore, several thriving export-oriented economic activities were located in Peru, and each was closely associated with European and North American penetration. Regrettably, however, they had little positive impact on Peru's long-term prospects for economic growth or for reducing social and economic inequalities. The effects on consumer demand were very small. Wages were extremely low on the plantations. In the mining areas the workforce was relatively small, and even if the mining wages did raise the standard of living for some families, the overall effect on the national population was negligible. The coastal plantations needed little infrastructure, and apart from port facilities they created almost nothing of use to other economic activities. Although the development of new mines led to the construction of major railways, they were usually located away from areas suited to agriculture or manufacturing industry and so were of limited benefit to long-term economic growth. The effects of plantation and mining production on other investment in the country were reduced by the fact that these activities were in the hands of foreign companies and foreign businessmen, so that much of the revenue simply went abroad.

From the viewpoint of national development, the most important problem of Peru's foreign-owned mines and plantations was that they were 'enclaves': small areas functioning as separate economic systems and not interrelating effectively with the surrounding regions. The company generally managed virtually all aspects of the operation, including all its own supplies, installations and exports. Its activities therefore had little spin-off for the other sectors of the Peruvian economy. The only significant benefit was the payment of taxes to the Peruvian government. However, these funds were most likely to be spent on projects which helped the already well-off sectors of the population, particularly the armed forces and the wealthy residents of the capital city. In terms of social change, Peru's export production tended to reinforce the huge economic and social differences between the various classes of the population which had emerged in the colonial era.

All these comments apply to the similar kinds of production in the other South American countries: for example, to plantation agriculture in Ecuador, Colombia and Brazil, and to mining in Chile and Bolivia. The export of tropical agricultural commodities and mineral products usually failed to encourage any broad-based economic growth, or social change. Their chief benefits were first in terms of opening up large areas for settlement (e.g. the Guayas lowlands of Ecuador), and second in yielding much-needed government revenue.

South-East Brazil

A study of economic change in Brazil shows that under certain circumstances sub-tropical export agriculture, which is not based on foreign-owned plantations, can play an important role in long-term economic growth. The crop which has had the most beneficial effects on other sectors of the economy is coffee. It replaced gold and sugar as Brazil's boom product and principal export in the nineteenth century, and it has been the country's single most important export for most of the twentieth century.

Coffee first became an important crop in the 1830s, at a time when it was grown chiefly in the Paraiba Valley. In the second half of the nineteenth century, coffee cultivation was expanded in areas to the west and north of São Paulo, taking advantage of the plentiful rich land and the labour provided by the large-scale immigration from Europe. By 1914, the single state of São Paulo was producing nearly 70 per cent of the world's coffee. The role of foreign penetration in coffee production is clear from the importance of European labour. By 1920 European immigrants owned a quarter of rural properties in the state of São Paulo. Foreigners also provided much of the basic infrastructure. The increase of coffee production to meet demand depended particularly on the railways, most of which were either British-owned or British-financed (Fig. 2.6).

The expansion of coffee production contributed significantly to long-term economic growth for two major reasons. First, the harvesting and processing of coffee are simple and labour-intensive. As a result coffee can be grown on smallholdings, where it can be combined with the cultivation of food crops. Though Brazilian coffee production was at first exclusively based on plantations, the ending of slavery in 1888, and the occurrence of large-scale European immigration, combined to encourage production on smallholdings. In this way the profits from coffee production were spread more widely among the population, raising consumer demand, and stimulating many kinds of domestic production. In Colombia, where coffee production grew to importance in the 1870s, coffee was from the beginning a smallholders' crop and, as in Brazil, contributed significantly to economic growth in the regions of cultivation. Under the plantation system, which has dominated the production of most other export crops, large profits go to the owners while the labour force gains only its wages, which tend to be low. In contrast, the smallholdings provide more employment and spread the incomes earned among a much larger number of people.

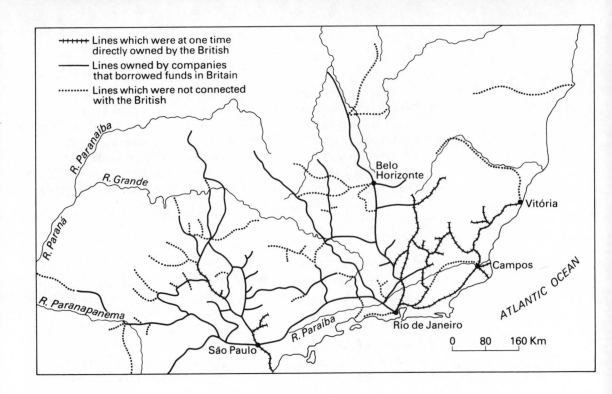

Fig. 2.6 The railway network of South-East Brazil by 1918, showing the role of British companies and British finance in their construction.

The second reason, more specific to the Brazilian case, is that the coffee cultivation extended over a very wide area with considerable agricultural potential, and was accompanied by the construction of an excellent railway system (Fig. 2.6) and good port facilities. Thus, unlike the cases of guano, sugar and minerals in Peru, coffee led to the creation of an infrastructure which was very useful to other types of production. The railways and harbours built to serve the coffee-export economy could also be used for distributing Brazilian manufactured goods. The railways, in particular, made São Paulo the centre of a regional market, and stimulated the growth of manufacturing industry in the city (see Chapter 4).

The Pampas of Argentina and Uruguay

Argentina and Uruguay are the South American countries which became major exporters of temperate farming products, an activity which encouraged broad-based economic growth. During the nineteenth century, Europe's growing demand for raw materials and foodstuffs stimulated a huge expansion of farming, and a significant population growth (Fig. 2.7). The traditional large landholding (estancia) of the colonial era had produced mainly cattle hides. This gave way to salt-beef production and then, during the mid-nineteenth century, sheep rearing became important. Up to the 1880s, hides, salted beef and wool were the principal exports, but during that decade they were overtaken by cereals, frozen mutton and beef. New technology, immigrants and substantial investments changed the Pampas into a region of cereal cultivation and quality stock raising. This change relied on the introduction of wire fencing to control the movement of cattle and sheep, refrigeration to enable the export of frozen meat to Europe, and railways to take the

Fig. 2.7 Baling alfalfa on a farm in Chubut, Argentina. This province, lying just to the south of the Pampas, was settled by Welsh and other Europeans during the late nineteenth century. Horses are used to work the machine which probably dates from before 1900. Alfalfa is a fodder for the thousands of sheep reared for their wool.

Fig. 2.8 The Argentine railway network in 1950.

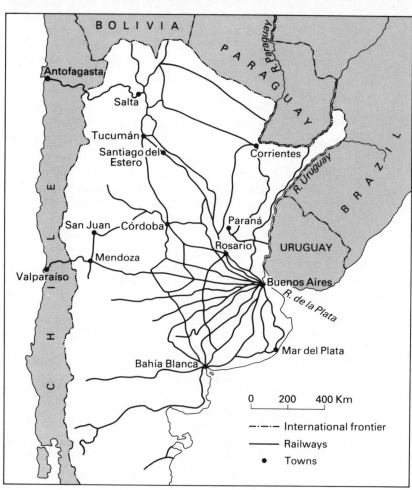

products to port. The British built a network of railways across the Pampas, providing the necessary infrastructure for future economic growth (Fig. 2.8), and they operated the major shipping services between

35

Argentina and Europe. Foreign penetration also took the form of large-scale immigration from Europe. Many of the tenant-farmers and wage labourers on the estancias were Europeans, and almost all the meat-packing plants, tanning factories and flour mills were established by European immigrants. Unlike the mines in Peru and Bolivia, however, these plants remained under family rather than corporate control, so that revenues generally remained in Argentina and Uruguay, rather than disappearing abroad.

The characteristics of the Argentinian and Uruguayan economies were favourable to their long-term growth. The Pampas had abundant fertile land which was relatively flat and well-watered, and the initial population density was very low. Although several million European immigrants were attracted to the region, the expansion of the economy was so rapid that labour remained in short supply. As the region did not have a strong tradition of labour exploitation through black slavery or Indian servitude, wages were fairly high. Overall, therefore, there was substantial local consumer demand, both because most of the production was in the hands of owners living in the region (as opposed to foreign companies exporting their profits), and because of the workers' capacity to buy a wide variety of goods. This demand stimulated trade in consumer goods, increasing the use of the region's extensive transport infrastructure and stimulating further employment.

The nineteenth century saw South America become a major world supplier of raw materials and foodstuffs, and an equally significant importer of industrial goods. The rise of these primary-product exporting economies owed much to foreign penetration, and particularly to foreign technology, investment and immigration. In those areas where foreign companies established plantations and mines as local enclaves, for example in Peru and Bolivia, there was little stimulus to regional or national economic development. Such plantations and mines generally made little contribution to local funds for investment, to the growth of consumer demand, to the encouragement of business skills, or to the creation of a transport infrastructure for regional development. In contrast, in those areas where there was a major expansion of medium- and small-scale farming for the export market, as in South-East Brazil and the Pampas, a major contribution was made in these directions. By the early twentieth century, therefore, the Pampas and South-East Brazil were in a far better position to industrialize than other regions of South America where the main exports were minerals or tropical plantation crops.

Population expansion

The economic changes of the colonial era, and of the first century following independence were accompanied by major population changes. After the conquest there was a huge decline in the indigenous Indian population, but by the eighteenth century population growth was occurring in most regions. The conquest also started the process of racial mixing, which has continued to the present day. During the nineteenth century, the world demand for primary products stimulated the spread of settlement into many previously empty regions of the continent.

Economic expansion, particularly in areas with abundant potential farmland and a temperate climate, attracted massive immigration and increasing rates of population growth.

During the twentieth century, any discussion of development increasingly relates to population trends. Since the 1940s most of the tropical countries of South America have been experiencing a population explosion and in some countries the growth of population has been faster than the growth of production for periods of several years at a time. The problems associated with this massive population increase will be discussed in other chapters. Here we will simply identify the characteristics of the population expansion.

The population of any country changes according to the operation of the four principal components: births, deaths, immigration and emigration. If there are more births and more immigrants than deaths and emigrants, the population expands. The population of South America has grown significantly since the early nineteenth century for two main reasons. First, there has been a large immigration into some regions; and second, a more important reason, the number of deaths has fallen drastically in relation to the number of births, particularly since 1940.

International migration

International migration during the nineteenth and early twentieth centuries had little effect on population growth in much of South America, but had a huge impact in Argentina, Uruguay and Brazil. In Brazil international migration was at first dominated by the slave trade which reached a peak between 1841 and 1850, when more than 338,000 African slaves were imported into the country. In Brazil's first national census of 1872, three-fifths of the inhabitants were Negroes or mulattos. By the year of the census, however, immigration from Europe was already affecting the racial composition of Brazil, particularly in the southern region. Between 1884 and 1954 Brazil received 4.6 million immigrants from Europe, most of them coming from Italy and Portugal.

In the River Plate area records of the flow of immigrants show that 3.4 million entered Argentina between 1881 and 1935, and almost 650,000 entered Uruguay over the same period. Here the largest groups were Italian and Spanish. Not all migrants became permanent settlers, of course, and there was a large return-flow. Nevertheless, in Argentina, Uruguay, South and South-East Brazil and to a lesser extent Chile, European migrants contributed significantly to the overall population expansion. In the 1914 population census, 30 per cent of the residents of Argentina had been born outside the country. A rather different case of international migration is Venezuela: there the immigration of southern Europeans since the 1910s has been followed since the 1940s by a huge in-flow of Colombians, mainly attracted by the relative prosperity of Venezuela and the labour shortages associated with an oil-boom economy. More than two million Colombians have moved to Venezuela, most of them illegally, in the hopes of finding higher-paid jobs.

Natural increase

All over the continent the death rate (the number of deaths per thousand population) began to fall in the century following independence. The introduction of clean piped water supplies and covered sewers in the cities, particularly from the late nineteenth century onwards, reduced the death rate in the urban areas. The greatest fall in the death rate occurred in the 1940s, when antibiotics and other medical advances, as well as the widespread use of insecticides to reduce insect-borne diseases, had a dramatic effect. Vast numbers of babies who would previously have died in infancy, now survived.

Although the death rate fell, the birth rate (the number of births per thousand population) remained at the same high level (Table 2.1). The large surplus of births over deaths resulted in a huge natural increase.

Table 2.1   Average annual birth and death rates per thousand by country 1950–1985

Country		1950–55	1960–65	1970–75	1980–85
Argentina	BR	25.4	23.2	23.4	24.6
	DR	9.2	8.8	9.0	8.7
Bolivia	BR	47.1	46.1	45.4	44.0
	DR	24.0	21.4	18.9	15.8
Brazil	BR	44.6	42.1	33.7	30.6
	DR	15.1	12.3	9.7	8.4
Chile	BR	35.8	36.4	27.0	22.7
	DR	13.8	11.8	8.6	6.7
Colombia	BR	47.6	44.6	33.3	31.0
	DR	16.4	12.2	9.0	7.7
Ecuador	BR	46.8	45.6	41.2	36.8
	DR	18.9	14.3	11.2	8.1
Guyana	BR	48.1	40.4	32.5	28.5
	DR	13.5	8.6	7.6	5.9
Paraguay	BR	45.5	42.2	37.5	36.0
	DR	15.4	11.9	8.1	7.2
Peru	BR	47.1	46.3	40.5	36.7
	DR	21.6	17.6	12.8	10.7
Uruguay	BR	21.2	21.9	21.1	19.5
	DR	10.5	9.6	10.0	10.2
Venezuela	BR	47.0	44.2	36.1	33.0
	DR	12.4	9.2	6.5	5.6

Suriname and French Guiana are omitted.

Source: United Nations, *Statistical Yearbook for Latin America 1985*.

When the birth rate was 40 per thousand per annum and the death rate 35 per thousand per annum, the natural increase was only 5 per 1,000; with the same birth rate, and a lower death rate of 15 per thousand per annum, the rate of natural increase became 25 per 1,000. Most South American countries have had birth and death rates at these levels at some period in the twentieth century. The extent of natural increase can be expressed in a variety of ways, but the basic message is clear: a significant natural increase results in major population growth.

The demographic transition

When describing population changes, it is common to refer to the 'demographic transition' which is a model of four stages of change in the

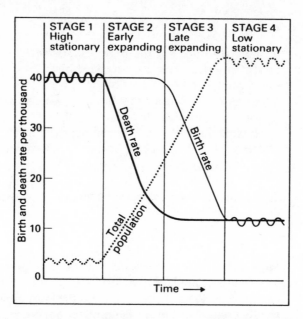

Fig. 2.9 The classic demographic transition model.

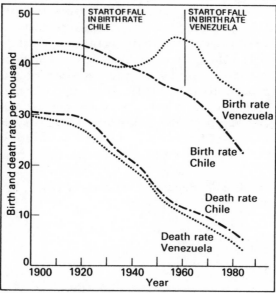

Fig. 2.10 The trend of birth rates and death rates in Chile and Venezuela 1900–85, showing that the birth rate begins to fall before the death rate has stabilized at a low level. This is different from stage 3 in the classic demographic transition model.
Sources: N. Sanchez-Albornoz, *The Population of Latin America*, University of California Press (1974); United Nations, CEPAL, *Statistical Yearbook for Latin America 1985*.

birth and death rates (Fig. 2.9). In the first stage, birth and death rates are both high, so that the population remains nearly stationary. In the second stage, called the early expanding phase, the birth rate continues to be high but the death rate falls. In the third stage, the late expanding stage, the birth rate falls while the death rate remains relatively low. In the final stage, the low stationary stage, both birth and death rates stay at a low level. In terms of total population growth the model suggests that after a period of rapid population growth due to a fall in the death rate, the following fall in the birth rate eventually results in a stationary population. Although most countries in Western Europe have reached the final stage, and have relatively stable populations, most South American countries are just entering the late expanding stage. Although the death rate has fallen substantially in all South American countries, the birth rate in most countries remains relatively high. By 1985 only three countries, Argentina, Uruguay and Chile, showed a significant and sustained decline in the birth rate. For the period 1980–1985, these were the only three South American countries to have birth rates under 25 per thousand. In these countries, the transition has probably been helped by the large-scale immigration of Europeans, bringing with them the twentieth-century, European preference for small families.

Most of the other South American countries, in particular Brazil, Colombia and Venezuela, began to experience a declining birth rate in the late 1960s and early 1970s. It is still uncertain, however, whether this decline in birth rate will be sustained long enough for most of the South American countries to pass completely into the final stage of the demographic transition.

The population explosion

High rates of natural increase, together with immigration in some regions, have led to a population explosion. Until the 1930s, the temperate countries of South America showed the most rapid population increase, chiefly because of European immigration, but since then tropical South America has surged ahead. The figures in Table 2.2 reveal the extent of the expansion. Since 1900, national populations have increased, varying from country to country, between 3.3 and 9.3 times.

In addition to the population explosion, there has been a change in population distribution, both between regions and also between the countryside and the cities. The regions with the most flourishing economies have experienced the greatest population growth. The changing population distribution has also involved the rapid growth of cities. As Chapter 5 explains, most population growth has been concentrated in the cities rather than in the countryside.

Table 2.2   Population by country 1850–1985 (in millions)

Country	1850	1900	1950	1985
Argentina	1.1	4.7	17.1	30.5
Bolivia	1.4	1.7	3.0	6.4
Brazil	7.2	17.3	52.3	135.6
Chile	1.3	2.9	6.1	12.1
Colombia	2.2	3.8	11.6	28.4
Ecuador	0.8	1.4	3.2	9.4
Paraguay	0.5	0.4	1.3	3.7
Peru	1.9	3.8	8.0	18.6
Uruguay	0.1	0.9	2.2	3.0
Venezuela	1.5	2.3	5.3	17.3

The figures are approximate. For the two countries omitted the 1985 population estimates are 790,000, Guyana and 393,000, Suriname.

Sources: N. Sanchez Albornoz, *The Population of Latin America*, University of California Press (1974); World Bank, *World Development Report 1987*.

3 The agrarian problems and dilemmas

Agriculture is of crucial importance to the South American economies, supplying food and industrial raw materials for domestic consumption and export. It is closely connected with the industrial and service sectors of the economy. Money earned in agriculture can be invested in non-agricultural sectors and, even more important, money earned by farmers can be used for purchasing the products of the non-agricultural sectors.

Through the case studies of South-East Brazil and the Pampas, the last chapter drew attention to the importance of agriculture in economic growth. This importance has continued in the twentieth century, and is demonstrated by statistics on GDP and exports. As Chapter 1 explains, GDP relates to the total value of goods and services produced or consumed within the national economy during a single year. In 1985, there were only three South American countries where agriculture contributed less than 10 per cent of GDP: Chile, Suriname and Venezuela (Table 3.1). On the other hand, there were three countries where agriculture yielded more than 20 per cent of GDP: Colombia, Guyana, and Paraguay. In 1983 more than 65 per cent of the export earnings of Argentina, Colombia and Paraguay derived from agriculture, and in Brazil, Guyana and Uruguay agriculture contributed more than 40 per cent of the value of exports. The

Table 3.1 The contribution of agriculture to GDP, exports and employment by country

Country	Value added to GDP by agriculture in 1985 (millions of 1986 US$)	Agriculture as % of GDP in 1985	Value of export of agricultural commodities as % of total value of exports 1983	% of economically active population in agriculture 1980
Brazil	34,296	10.7	41.5	31
Argentina	9,719	14.0	75.3	13
Colombia	7,973	21.7	68.0	34
Peru	3,539	15.2	6.9	40
Venezuela	3,496	7.3	0.8	16
Chile	2,565	9.6	9.3	17
Paraguay	1,872	26.9	91.6	49
Ecuador	1,752	13.9	17.0	39
Bolivia	1,237	19.6	5.4	46
Uruguay	840	11.1	64.9	16
Guyana	143	23.4	56.5	–
Suriname	97	8.7	–	–

Sources: Inter-American Development Bank, *1987 Report*; United Nations, *Statistical Yearbook for Latin America 1985, 1986*; World Bank, *World Development Report 1987*.

countries with the lowest agricultural exports relative to other exports are Bolivia, Chile, Suriname and Venezuela, all of which are major exporters of minerals or petroleum products.

The problem of food production

The population of South America has expanded dramatically in the last few decades, and this has led to an increased demand for food and the urgent need to expand food production. Over the period 1965–1984, however, only five of the ten major South American countries improved their per capita food production (Table 3.2). Although as much as a third of the working population of the continent is still employed in agriculture, food production has rarely grown as rapidly as GDP and many of the South American countries are now net importers of staple foods. The export of such agricultural commodities as coffee, cocoa, bananas, cane sugar, beef and soya continues to be very significant, and the expansion of production for export is reflected in the high growth rates of agricultural production of such countries as Brazil and Paraguay. However, much of the revenue earned now has to be spent on the import of such basic foods as wheat and maize. For example, although more than half of South American countries were self-sufficient in wheat and maize in 1965, only Argentina retained this position in 1984 (Table 3.3). In Brazil, wheat imports increased $2^{1}/_{2}$ times between 1965 and 1984, and the country changed from the position of maize exporter to maize importer. While the pattern of imports fluctuates slightly from year to year, according to changes in world prices and the influence of climate on harvest size, the overall trend towards higher dependence on grain imports is clear. Many other food crops show a similar trend. Venezuela, for example, was self-sufficient in sugar as recently as the 1960s, but in

Table 3.2 Changes in per capita food production and the growth of agricultural production by country

Countries ranked in descending order of index change	Per capita food production index (1965–69 = 100)		Average annual growth rate (%) of agricultural production
	1974–76	1982–84	1973–84
Brazil	114	131	4.0
Uruguay	110	116	1.5
Argentina	104	113	1.6
Colombia	106	110	3.5
Bolivia	119	100	1.1
Venezuela	113	99	2.4
Paraguay	94	99	5.7
Chile	92	94	3.4
Ecuador	97	86	1.6
Peru	99	83	1.2

Guyana and Suriname are omitted.
Food production relates to cereals, starchy roots, sugar, pulses, edible oil crops, nuts, fruits, vegetables, wine, cocoa, livestock and livestock products.

Sources: World Bank, *World Development Report 1978, 1986.*

Table 3.3 Wheat and maize trade by country 1965 and 1984. (Net exports are shown in italics; all other figures are net imports.)

Country	Wheat and wheat flour (hundred metric tons)		Maize (hundred metric tons)	
	1965	1984	1965	1984
Argentina	*66,716*	*73,711*	*28,038*	*55,183*
Bolivia	—	2,697	—	—
Brazil	18,857	48,676	*5,597*	781
Chile	2,752	9,724	—	362
Colombia	1,735	6,606	—	104
Ecuador	—	2,450	—	—
Guyana	—	67	—	—
Paraguay	—	750	—	—
Peru	4,556	9,845	—	1,150
Suriname	—	260	—	150
Uruguay	—	*234*	—	36
Venezuela	5,569	9,677	—	13,228

Sources: Food and Agriculture Organization of the United Nations (FAO), *Monthly Bulletin of Agricultural Economics and Statistics*, 17, no. 11 (November 1968); FAO, *Monthly Bulletin of Statistics*, 9, no. 3 March (1986).

1980, 60 per cent of domestic sugar consumption had to be met by imported sugar.

The relative decline in the production of many staple foods in South America is due to four major factors, in addition to that of rapid population expansion. First, since the 1940s, both the governments and the private sector have concentrated their investments on construction, industrialization, public services and the purchase of land in the major cities. As a result, agriculture has received little investment in relation to its enormous importance as an employer of labour, and to its role as a food producer and export earner. Indeed, many of the profits made in agriculture have been invested in urban activities, producing a major flow of funds from rural to urban areas. Second, governments have tended to hold down the price of foodstuffs in order to prevent large rises in the cost of living, and to win or retain the political support of those who live in the cities and have to purchase their food. As a result, the profitability of the agricultural sector has been reduced and investment in food production has been deterred. Third, what investment there has been in agriculture has tended to be for the production of crops for industrial use and export. These crops have generally fetched higher prices than basic food commodities. As a result, the South American countries have concentrated on the production of export crops, mainly for consumption in the richer North American and Western European countries, while neglecting the production of essential foodstuffs for their own populations. Fourth and last, most South American countries have imported large amounts of grain from the United States and Canada, partly through purchase at relatively low prices, and partly as 'food aid' in the form of gifts or highly subsidised loans. Such 'dumping' of North American food surpluses in South American markets has acted as a severe disincentive to local producers. These producers cannot compete and many eventually decide that it is better to shift their labour and savings into another sector of the economy, such as urban property and commerce.

The need to import substantial amounts of food accentuates the foreign trade problems of most South American countries. Large outflows of foreign currency are required to pay interest and repay capital on existing foreign debts, and when many foods, manufactures and services must also be imported, the foreign exchange earned through exports is insufficient to cover requirements. Under these circumstances, food is already posing a serious balance-of-payments problem for such countries as Peru and Chile. In other words these countries are having difficulty in balancing their foreign spending with their foreign earnings, and have to borrow further money to pay for imports. The problem is made worse because, of all the South American countries, only Colombia, Peru, Venezuela and Ecuador are self-sufficient in oil. Many countries therefore have to import oil and food, particularly as oil for making fertilizers and fuelling agricultural vehicles is essential if food production is to be increased.

The problem of inadequate food production is also linked with the inefficient use of land resources. Less than 10 per cent of the continent's surface is cultivated, and policies to expand the cultivated area have generally not been given a high priority. Brazil, for example, has vast stretches of land, particularly savannah, which have hardly begun to be used. In order to open up these and other areas, transport links and store facilities need to be built, and the new farmers need to be provided with legal titles to the land and practical assistance on farming methods. With a long history of investment concentrated in the cities, however, it is difficult to switch attention to the countryside.

The characteristics of South American agriculture

Almost every crop and every type of livestock is found somewhere in South America, for the great variety of environmental conditions contributes to a very varied agriculture. Within this variety it is common to identify two generalized categories of farming, the traditional and the modern.

In traditional farming the techniques of cultivation and land tenure reflect the customs of many centuries (Fig. 3.1). Land tenure refers to the way the land is held, whether it is in large or small units and whether it is owned or rented. Traditional farming includes the large estates introduced by the Spanish and Portuguese, and also the many smallholdings in such regions as North-East Brazil and the Andean Highlands. In the Andes, the Indians who own small plots often also have access to common land owned by the community as a whole. The common land is generally used for grazing livestock, and the individual plots are cultivated, mostly for subsistence needs. The Indian land is usually limited to the poorer and more isolated areas because the best farming land was taken over by the Spaniards (Fig. 3.2).

The large traditional farming estates have survived from the colonial period in the two principal forms described in the last chapter: the hacienda and the plantation. The hacienda is a feature of the Andes, the

Fig. 3.1 Traditional farming methods near the town of Cajamarca in the Andes of northern Peru. Cattle are used to pull a simple wooden plough. A woman scatters seed by hand.

Fig. 3.2 Farmland near the town of Riobamba in the Andes of Ecuador. Most of the hacienda land in the foreground is used as pasture, while the small-holdings on the steep, eroded hillside are intensively cultivated.

Brazilian Highlands, and north-east Argentina, although in the last two regions respectively the terms fazenda and estancia are used to describe this type of estate. The hacienda is generally noted both for the hardship and poverty suffered by its tenants and labourers, and for its inefficient farming. The owner is often more concerned with the social status and financial security provided by the hacienda than with the income it might yield. As a result, modernization of these estates has been slow. The plantation belongs to the tropical lowlands and produces crops for export. The traditional plantation continues to be organized like its colonial predecessor, relying on cheap wage-labour and the simplest forms of mechanization and processing. Increasingly, however, these plantations are being converted to the use of modern technology and management methods, and hence to the category of modern farming.

Modern farming has emerged since the mid-nineteenth century and is more closely concerned with the production of goods for sale. It is

45

responsive to change and ready to adopt new agricultural practices, and it includes two principal types: the family farm and the industrial plantation. The family farm is found chiefly in Argentina, Uruguay and southern Brazil, regions which received large numbers of European immigrants in the late nineteenth and early twentieth centuries. Family farms chiefly grow crops to sell and they are usually efficiently run, operating with the labour of the family itself. A far more significant type of modern farming is the industrial plantation, which can be described as an agribusiness (see later section in this chapter). Industrial plantations have expanded rapidly since the 1960s, particularly in many tropical coastal zones and in the forested lands of the Amazon Basin. Such plantations involve a heavy investment in processing plants and irrigation, and in order to operate economically they require large areas of land, often producing only one type of crop. In contrast to many traditional estates, the large size of the modern plantation contributes to its efficiency.

Recognition of the variations in South American agriculture, with its traditional and modern farming systems and their varying emphasis on subsistence and commercial production, points to some of the major agrarian dilemmas. The government policy-makers need to achieve an appropriate balance between the different farming systems. Efficiency of production should be weighed against the welfare of the rural population. Modern plantations, for example, might encourage high agricultural production, but possess social disadvantages because they rely on a few large landowners and a mass of landless wage-labourers. In many traditional farming areas, the present mix of large estates and smallholdings seems to satisfy neither the economic objectives of securing maximum agricultural production nor the social objectives of achieving maximum social justice. Another problem is to find a balance between production for export and the production of subsistence crops and commodities for the local market. Many modern plantations, while producing for export and therefore earning foreign exchange, do nothing to lessen the dependence of some South American countries on food imports. The dilemmas involved in balancing the various priorities of agricultural change become clear when we examine two of the major features and trends in the rural areas: first, the existence of major inequalities in land distribution and the associated quest for land reform; and second, and more recently, the growth of agribusiness.

Rural inequalities: land distribution

Despite recent reforms, South America is still characterized by a land distribution in which most of the land is concentrated into a few hands. Because of the widespread existence of large holdings, a very small proportion of a country's landowners controls most of the useful land. In Ecuador the 1968 Agricultural Census showed that only just over 1 per cent of all farm holdings were larger than 100 hectares, but the few privileged owners of those holdings controlled 47 per cent of all Ecuador's farm land. Because so much of the land is in so few hands it follows that the majority of rural dwellers are either landless or own very little land. One-third of all farm holdings in Ecuador were smaller than one hectare. The owners of these smallholdings, even though there were

Fig. 3.3 A cluster of smallholders' huts and tiny fields to the south of Riobamba in the Andes of Ecuador.

so many of them, together held a mere 1 per cent of Ecuador's farm land. In Ecuador, as in most South American countries, there is a mass of poor farmers and farm workers alongside a few wealthy landowners.

The high levels of inequality in land distribution in South America are more apparent in some regions than in others. In sparsely-populated tropical lowlands dominated by modern industrial plantations, the concentration of landownership is not such a problem, because there are very few smallholders. Here there is little pressure for farm land from the rural poor, simply because there are so few of them. The situation is entirely different in the highland regions where there is traditional farming. Here there is often a stark contrast between the large estates and the small plots cultivated by the hacienda workers or owned by Indian families. The following section will therefore focus on the inequalities existing in the traditional highland regions of the continent, where rural population expansion has increased the pressure for land.

Smallholders with only a few hectares or less usually have a struggle to survive (Fig. 3.3). They cultivate their land intensively and acquire outside jobs where possible to increase their incomes. They will take temporary work on the local haciendas at harvest time or engage in part-time trading, perhaps selling foodstuffs in some of the nearby weekly markets. In much of the Andean Highlands and in North-East Brazil the smallholdings lie alongside the large estates, and it is here that the differences between the two types of holding are most evident.

The owner of the large estate generally possesses far more land than he would need to earn a comfortable income, even by First World standards. His house, as shown in Fig. 3.4, is typically a well-built two-storey, tile-roofed building with servants' quarters, very different from the straw-thatched, single-roomed mud huts of many smallholders (Fig. 3.5). He will have several motor vehicles as well as horses, while the smallholder possesses no means of transport other than his own two legs. The owner of the large estate and the smallholder seem to live in different worlds.

The contrast in life styles is particularly clear on the traditional haciendas of the Andean Highlands, which usually have relied on the labour of large numbers of Indian workers. Until the land reforms of the 1950s in Bolivia and the 1960s and 1970s in Peru and Ecuador, most of

Fig. 3.4 Hacienda Cañas Gordas near the city of Cali, Colombia. This wealthy eighteenth-century hacienda house lies in an area of sugar-cane cultivation and cattle ranching.

Fig. 3.5 An Indian smallholder's thatched-roof house (right) and haystack (left), near Riobamba. In the foreground three donkeys are being driven around in a circle in order to thresh barley spread on the ground, through the stamping of their hoofs.

the Indian labour force was resident on the hacienda. These Indians exchanged their labour for the right to cultivate small portions of the hacienda's land for their own subsistence. Not only did they provide agricultural labour and mind livestock for the hacienda-owner, but they also provided a variety of personal services including domestic duties in his residence. Traditional hacienda production also relied to some extent on sharecroppers. These were tenants who were allowed to cultivate a small area of the estate in return for supplying the landowner with a fixed proportion of the harvest. There were also wage-workers on the estates, who were often employed only intermittently, and were sometimes paid in food (such as potatoes and maize) produced on the estate. Largely as a result of the land reforms, only a few of the surviving traditional haciendas in the Andes operate with a resident Indian labour force, exchanging access to land for labour or shares of products. Instead, there has been a shift to the use of wage-workers, often from the smallholding communities close to the hacienda. These wage-workers are usually poor smallholders or landless labourers who are prepared to take casual employment. The wages paid by the haciendas are usually very low, and work is generally only available at sowing and harvest times.

The hacienda worker, whatever the form of his tenancy or employment, is always much poorer than the landowner. A study in Chile in the 1950s showed that the annual income of the owner was between 80 and 218 times as much as the income of the workers. The hacienda workers were also, at least until recent changes in legislation, in a precarious position, with no formal labour contracts or rights to the plots of land on which they lived. Although they had no security they could still be tied like serfs to the estates, often because of their financial debts to the landowner. The contrast between landlord and worker is as great in social terms as it is economically. The landlord is a powerful figure in local and national society, while the hacienda worker occupies the lowliest position. At the same time, however, the landlord has traditionally been a father-figure and protector, treating his workers like children and providing such services as first-aid, and perhaps securing their release from gaol should they get into trouble with the police. This small protection given to the estate worker should not, however, obscure the basic oppression of the traditional hacienda.

The disadvantages of gross inequality in land distribution

The gross inequality of land distribution is an obstacle to economic growth and the improvement of social welfare. First, both the hacienda and the smallholding are wasteful of resources. The traditional hacienda is often owned mainly for status and security against inflation, and it is usually inefficiently farmed. The landowner frequently lives away from the hacienda and often fails to take an active interest in its productivity. Providing the hacienda gives him a comfortable income he does not worry if large sections of his holding lie unused, so that yields per hectare are usually low. From an economic viewpoint, therefore, the traditional hacienda is an obstacle to growth in agricultural production.

While the hacienda is wasteful of land because areas suitable for cultivation are left almost unused, the smallholding can be wasteful of land and labour. Smallholders generally spend most of their working time intensively cultivating plots which are often widely scattered. The value of their production, however, is relatively low in relation to the large amounts of labour that they put in. They usually do not have the money or land necessary for using modern methods of cultivation. Even more of a problem is that the intensive cultivation of the land reduces soil fertility and encourages deforestation and erosion. Many of the plots should be left under trees or pasture, but because they are the owners' only source of livelihood they are used instead to produce food crops. As a result, the top soil loses its fertility, the plots become bare and the soil is washed away (Fig. 3.6). In regions like North-East Brazil, as a result of population pressure, intensively cultivated smallholdings have been established on land which is distant from the rivers. Without a source of irrigation water, such plots have proved to be very vulnerable when the rains fail. Drought has devastated the crops on the smallholdings and much of the land has been ruined by soil erosion when the rains

Fig. 3.6 Environmental deterioration on the western slopes of the Andes, in central Ecuador. Landslips, slumping, some gullying and sheet erosion have resulted from the over-cultivation of the steep slopes.

eventually came. In this way, smallholdings have encouraged the wastage of land because the plots are over-cultivated, and the land may be rendered useless for cultivation.

A second reason why the grossly unequal land distribution is an obstacle to economic growth is that it can slow down industrial expansion. In order for industrialization to take place, there need to be people willing and able to buy the goods produced. Where there are a few rich estate owners and a mass of very poor people who are either landless or who cultivate smallholdings, the only people who can afford to buy many industrial goods are the wealthy estate owners. Their incomes are so high that they tend to buy imported luxury goods. Because so few can afford to buy these goods, and because many of the goods are very sophisticated and expensive to manufacture, there is little possibility of the industries which produce these elite consumption goods being established in most South American countries. At the other extreme those earning wages on the large estates or those cultivating smallholdings can only earn enough to supply their basic needs, and not enough to buy many industrial goods. The mass of rural poor, therefore, cannot become part of the domestic market necessary for the growth of new industries. In this way the concentration of land and therefore wealth in a few hands, holds back industrial growth because most people are too poor to become consumers of the products that industry might manufacture.

A third reason is that the grossly unequal land distribution is an obstacle to the improvement of living conditions for most of the rural poor. Particularly in the Andean Highlands and North-East Brazil, the traditional haciendas subjected much of the rural population to a miserable life. They treated their workers badly, and often they deprived the neighbouring smallholding communities of much of their livelihood by taking over some of their land or by denying them access to water supplies or communal pasture. Most of the rural population, therefore, are too poor to adequately feed, clothe and house themselves, or to take advantage of health care and educational opportunities. Furthermore, most governments have given relatively little attention to providing schools, clinics and other public services in rural areas, and the hacienda-owners have often prevented their workers from using the available facilities. The result is that most of the rural population in areas with traditional haciendas and smallholding communities have very low levels of education and are effectively denied an active role in national life.

In areas with large haciendas, where there are gross inequalities in land distribution and obvious inefficiencies in agriculture, there have been numerous calls for the redistribution of land and the reorganization of production. Smallholders and landless workers have become increasingly discontented as they have become more aware of the better living and working conditions available in the cities and in other countries. The growing discontent has led to strikes, blockades and the occupation of estates, and to armed reprisals by the landowners. In the 1950s and early 1960s, the situation was particularly explosive in North-East Brazil, central Colombia and highland Peru, and in the 1980s rural civil unrest is widespread again in Colombia and Peru. In response to this unrest, most governments have made at least a token attempt at reducing inequalities through land reform, and all have stated their concern for 'rural development' and improving the welfare of the rural poor. In many cases, however, police or troops have been sent to stop disturbances or hunt down revolutionaries and some of the rural poor have been injured, imprisoned or killed as a result. In some parts of Colombia and Peru, virtual civil war has broken out in some rural areas.

The frustrated quest for land reform

Land reform involves a change in the pattern of landownership whereby large estates are either converted to co-operative farms or subdivided into medium-sized farms and smallholdings. The latter is the most common type of land reform in South America, and it is normally achieved by government compulsory purchase of the estates. The large estates are then divided amongst the estate workers, who usually purchase the land by instalments from the government land reform agency. Such a change requires government legislation (a land reform law), particularly as the former landowners are usually paid considerably less than market prices for the land which is taken from them.

In theory, land reform solves most of the problems described in the previous pages. The aims of land reform are to encourage the expansion and modernization of agriculture, to assist industrialization, and to reduce some of the social and economic inequalities in traditional farming areas. In practice, however, land reform is extremely difficult to administer, and its aims are rarely achieved. Large landowners do not want to lose their land and because they are usually one of the groups with most power and status in their countries, governments are reluctant to push through measures which go against the landowners' wishes. The fact that the rural poor would benefit from land reform is not the main concern to the governments of countries where the mass of population has little power and influence. The introduction and extent of land reform depends on the government. It is only in countries where the poor have acquired significant political influence, or where the government is determined to win mass support, that real land reform has taken place.

By 1950 no land reform had been carried out in South America even though nearby Mexico had experienced land reform from 1915 onwards. By 1965, most South American countries had introduced some land reform legislation. Even by 1980, however, only Bolivia and Peru had undergone a significant and apparently lasting land reform, though there had also been some important changes in Chile and Ecuador. Elsewhere, the legislation has had only small impact.

The impact of land reform is best examined in the countries where it has been fairly comprehensive. In Bolivia, land reform was introduced after the 1952 revolution brought a sympathetic government to power. During the revolution, many haciendas were taken over by the workers and this action was later legalized by the 1953 land reform law. The 1953 law decreed that all large estates, with the exception of the efficiently-run industrial plantations, were to be divided up amongst those who cultivated them. The landlords often received no payment for their estates, while the former tenants and sharecroppers often obtained the land free. At a fairly typical hacienda close to Lake Titicaca, land reform meant the take-over of all 157 hectares and their subdivision amongst fifty hacienda workers. Each of the fifty received between 2 and 6 hectares of land. Thirty-two of the individuals were former hacienda tenants who had cultivated plots on the estate. The other eighteen, although living on the estate, did not have their own plots, and because of their lower status received less land after the reform than the hacienda tenants. The former owners of the hacienda who lived in the city of La Paz and in the local town were left without any of the hacienda land.

In Peru equally dramatic change occurred after a radical military government took power in 1968. Active land reform between 1969 and 1976 affected 47 per cent of Peru's agricultural land, and perhaps 38 per cent of the agricultural population. In contrast to Bolivia, the reform was not sparked off by the widespread illegal occupation of haciendas. Also in contrast, just over three-quarters of estate land affected by the reform, including most of the coastal plantations, has been reorganized into state-supported co-operative or collective units (Fig. 3.7). The original intention was for each co-operative or collective unit to be run as a single large estate, with the unit having a share in decisions and receiving a share of the profits. In practice, however, this form of organization has generally only proved successful in the coastal plantations. On most of the former haciendas of the highlands, the workers have shown a strong desire to own their own land. Often, there has also been pressure for land from the smallholders and landless labourers in the communities bordering the estates. In many cases the highland estates have effectively been divided into smallholdings, and the co-operative model is generally unpopular.

Land reform has affected most South American countries to some degree. Almost everywhere legislation has improved the position of tenants, and in several countries sharecropping has been virtually eliminated. In some areas, however, such legislation has encouraged landlords to evict their tenants and, instead, to buy more machinery and hire day labourers for the operation of their estates. Where this has happened, the land reform legislation has indirectly worsened the situation of many rural dwellers. In parts of the continent, for example highland Ecuador, other factors are supporting the process of land redistribution. For example, the mere threat of having their estates

Fig. 3.7 Mechanized wheat harvesting on a co-operative farm in the Jequetepeque valley near the town of Pacasmayo in coastal Peru.

confiscated has encouraged many large landowners to sell off sections of their holdings, and others have sold off land in order to reinvest their money more profitably in the cities or in foreign countries.

Overall, the effects of land reform have been limited. The distribution of land in South America is still highly unequal, and the problem of large numbers of smallholders and landless remains. It is undoubtedly true that land reform has improved the lot of some of the rural poor. Those who now have land have greater security and are financially better off. In Bolivia between 1955 and 1967 nearly 200,000 families received land from the 7.9 million hectares distributed. Their social position has improved because much of the hardship and uncertainty of their lives on the traditional haciendas has been swept away. But those rural dwellers not resident on the large estates have usually failed to benefit from land reform. If we evaluate land reform from the point of view of increasing the domestic market for industrial goods and promoting social justice, it is clear that it has achieved only modest improvements. Most of the rural poor, and particularly the communities of smallholders and landless labourers living away from the old haciendas and plantations, have been only marginally affected by the reforms. The positive impact of land reform on agricultural productivity has been very small. Most of the new landowners are unable to farm their new holdings efficiently because they lack the expertise and the money for basic machinery and other improvements. Much of the former hacienda land was pasture, and some of this has proved difficult and costly to convert into crop land. Before their land was taken over, some of the hacienda owners even deliberately reduced its usefulness by removing irrigation pumps, and by selling off all the breeding stock and farm machinery.

In order to be fully successful, land reform needs to be accompanied by technical and financial assistance. The new landowners need advice on pest control and fertilizers. Regrettably, the former landowners have often become traders and moneylenders, taking control of the supply of these modern agricultural inputs, and often making large profits at the expense of the new farmers. The former landowners also often control the marketing of the crops and animal products, again reaping large profits because they sell the goods at a far higher price than they paid the farmers. The new landowners need alternatives to these unscrupulous 'middlemen', just as they need money loans to purchase equipment and to construct irrigation systems. The impact of land reform on economic growth has been limited because of the lack of attention to these other needs. Land reform could have overcome the problem of extreme inequalities in the countryside, but the half-hearted or one-sided ways in which land reform has been carried out in most South American countries have doomed it to failure.

While land reform remains an ideal, it is no longer a key issue. South American governments were once fearful that rural unrest might lead on to national revolution. However, with the build-up of government military strength, combined with the major redistribution of population from rural to urban areas, this fear has diminished. Land conflicts now tend to be localized, and there is little prospect of their leading to national revolution. The pressures for reform are now so much weaker that little change in the land tenure structure is likely to occur in those rural areas where the land distribution remains highly unequal. The new key issue in the agrarian economy of South America is the role of agribusiness.

The growth of agribusiness

In contrast to land reform, which has reduced the number of large estates, a counter-trend in South American agriculture is the establishment of increasingly large agricultural enterprises. While land reform is a feature of traditional farming areas, the new large agricultural enterprise, or agribusiness, is a feature of modern farming regions, especially the tropical lowlands.

An agribusiness is a firm which may own or control any or all of the phases of agricultural production, from making fertilizers to operating plantations, and from processing crops to marketing the products. It is an agricultural enterprise run like a large industrial company. They first appeared in South America at the close of the nineteenth century, when North American companies set up sugar and banana plantations along the Pacific and Caribbean coasts. Such companies have come to be known as multinationals, because they operate in more than one country.

The real expansion of agribusiness did not start until the 1960s, when a huge surge of foreign investment led to the spread of these concerns. The trend was particularly pronounced in Brazil where, since the major change of government in 1964, foreign companies have been encouraged to establish agribusinesses in the Amazon Basin. One well-publicized venture is the Jari Forestry and Ranching Company, established by the American multi-millionaire, Daniel Ludwig, which began to open up over a million hectares in the late 1960s. By 1980, the Jari agribusiness included cattle zones, rice growing areas and commercial forest with an accompanying pulp factory, as well as a rice mill and kaolin plant (Fig. 3.8). The German Volkswagen and Italian Liquigas companies both opened huge cattle ranches in Brazilian Amazonia in the 1970s. Such firms have been attracted by the cheap land and labour available in the country, and by the opportunity to diversify their investments.

The growth of agribusiness has been associated with three principal trends, each of which shows the impact of agribusiness on the countries involved. The first is the growing concentration on export crops.

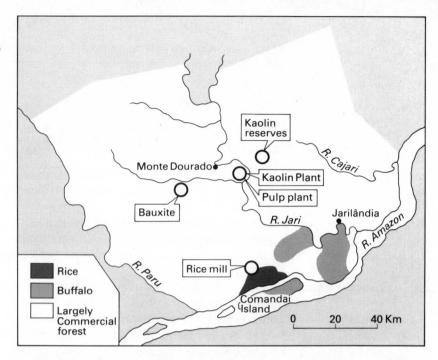

Fig. 3.8 The Jari agribusiness in Brazil. Source: *Latin America Regional Reports Brazil*, RB–81–01, 2 January 1981.

Agribusiness aims to produce crops which will yield the highest profits, and this often means growing crops for sale in the First World. Although agribusiness in Brazil produces such crops as manioc and sugar-cane for alcohol production to supply the home market, one of the major crops is soya for export. By 1977, Brazil's share of the world soya bean and meal market was 19 per cent. Since then, Brazil's export earnings from soya have almost equalled those from coffee, and in 1986 comprised 7 per cent of exports, compared with coffee's 9.2 per cent. Vast soya plantations were also established in neighbouring Paraguay in the 1970s, and here soya accounted for 19 per cent of exports in 1986, in second place to cotton. Concentration on export crops makes a country vulnerable to world changes in commodity prices. In addition, the growth of export agriculture is usually associated with a lower production of domestic food crops, because land formerly used for this purpose is often taken over by the new plantations. As a result of this and the large population expansion, the countries have to import essential foods. In Brazil the expansion of soya cultivation has contributed to a fall in the production of maize and black beans and the consequent rise in prices of these staple foods.

A second trend associated with the growth of agribusiness is the increasing size of the agricultural units. This is demonstrated in Brazil by the holdings of 1,000 hectares or more which covered 20 million more hectares of land in 1975 than in 1970, when they already accounted for 39 per cent of agricultural land (Table 3.4). Larger sugar mills are supplanting the small, and even in countries like Colombia, the larger coffee producers are flourishing at the expense of the small. Such a trend has many social disadvantages. The concentration of land and capital in a few hands makes the gulf between rich and poor far wider. People are driven off the land by the expanding agribusinesses which buy their holdings and leave them landless, or which simply take over holdings where the previous occupants did not have legal property titles. The displaced former smallholders usually either join the growing numbers of

Table 3.4   Agricultural landholdings in Brazil 1970

Size of landholdings ha	Landholdings		Area thousand	
	no.	%	ha	%
Under 10	2,524,982	51.4	9,111	3.1
10–99	1,935,130	39.0	60,163	20.1
100–999	415,224	8.5	108,910	37.2
1000 and over	37,163	0.8	114,829	39.2

Source: *Statistical Abstract of Latin America,* 20 (1980).

day labourers on the new estates, or migrate to the cities. Thus, where agribusiness is characterized by highly mechanized, modern plantations, there is a trend towards larger land units, and a displacement of the rural population.

A third principal trend associated with the growth of agribusiness is an increasing foreign domination of South American agricultural production. This foreign domination initially took the form of foreign-owned, modern plantations. However, from the late 1960s onwards, this became politically unacceptable in some countries and foreign-owned plantations have been taken over by the state. In Peru, the two largest US- and Dutch-controlled sugar agribusinesses were nationalized in 1969 and transferred to 'Agricultural Production Cooperatives', nominally controlled by their workers. Guyana took over the chief foreign sugar companies in 1975. Brazil is a major exception in the continent, because foreign agribusiness operating plantations and cattle ranches continues to be welcome, particularly as part of the drive to open up the Amazon Basin. In most other countries, although direct foreign control of production has ceased because of the nationalization of plantations, foreign agribusiness continues to dominate through its control of processing, marketing and trading. It is the large foreign companies which buy most of South America's sugar and coffee. The companies have vast resources and a good inside knowledge of the market, which allow them to buy the goods when the price is low, to stockpile, and then sell when the price goes up. In 1977, for example, one US company, General Foods (makers of Maxwell House), bought one-fifth of the coffee crop in Brazil. The situation is similar for bananas, and in Ecuador, for example, companies like United Brands buy up most of the banana exports. In general, it is the foreign companies which take most of the profit. A study of the banana trade in the early 1970s revealed that of every dollar's worth of bananas sold to US consumers, only 11 cents reached the producing country.

The impact of agribusiness

Successful agribusiness can assist economic growth by boosting export revenues but, as the previous comments have suggested, the economic advantages of agribusiness seem to be limited and very short-term. Agribusiness established in virtually unpopulated areas requires either heavy government investment in roads and other infrastructure, or total exemption from taxation on profits. The returns to the government from agribusinesses are generally very low, because the foreign control of such companies means that much of the revenue simply flows abroad. Concentration on export crops has been at the expense of food production for the local market. Moreover, the continued cultivation of a single crop without rotation usually causes soil deterioration, a problem which is particularly acute in the Amazon Basin. The social disadvantages accompanying the growth of agribusiness are especially clear. The concentration of wealth in agribusiness contrasts with the poverty of the peasants displaced by the expansion of the large landholdings. In addition, agribusiness is characterized by high mechanization and employs only a small proportion of the rural labour force. Those that do gain work as day-labourers are paid very low wages and have no job security. Others simply join the flow of migrants to the cities and add to the population of the urban slums.

The expansion of agribusiness has taken place despite the obvious disadvantages associated with the trend. The government supporters of agribusiness are attracted by the prospect of increased production by efficient and highly technological methods. They are not immediately aware of the problems which follow, due to the concentration on export rather than domestic food crops; the displacement of rural population by the huge agricultural units; and the foreign domination of production, processing and marketing. In drawing up policies relating to the expansion of agribusiness, just as in drawing up policies to tackle the problems of land distribution in the traditional farming areas, governments are faced with many dilemmas. Sound policies often involve sacrificing short-term economic gains to the cause of long-term social and economic advantages.

4 Dependent industrialization

Industrialization can be defined as the increase in the proportion of total GNP or GDP resulting from the manufacture of goods in factories. Industrial activity grows more rapidly than the economy as a whole, so that the proportional significance of industry increases. Many governments and economic policy makers see industrialization as the key to economic growth, and as a precondition for raising levels of income and employment. They cite the experiences of Western Europe, the United States, Japan and the Soviet Union as evidence that this is true. Most advocates of industrialization also argue that it provides more employment for the population and diversifies national economies which rely too heavily on a few primary exports.

The obstacles to industrialization in South America are considerable, with numerous problems resulting from the continent's position on the periphery, or edge of the world economy. The core areas of the world economy are the First World countries, and especially those of Western Europe, North America, and also Japan. They have a long history of industrialization and are at the centre of world communications. They have excellent information networks and the technology for efficient industrial production. As a result the core tends to dominate the periphery and to stifle its industrial development. The concepts of 'core' and 'periphery' can also be used in describing the uneven distribution of industrial growth within South America.

In addition to the major disadvantages stemming from their peripheral location, South American countries do not have sufficient infrastructure: the roads, railways, electric power, and other basic services which enable industry to function efficiently. Most countries also have shortages of appropriately skilled labour, of vital industrial fuels, and of the capital and managerial expertise necessary to get industries started. Furthermore, the size of the domestic market (the population within the country which is willing and able to buy the goods) is often extremely small, and the transport links to possible markets in neighbouring countries are generally poor. Alongside these various obstacles, the South American countries have the advantages of some useful raw materials and of relatively cheap labour when compared with the First World. It should be remembered however, that most available labour is unskilled, and that the cost of labour is higher than in many Asian countries.

Each of the South American countries has experienced a small degree of industrialization, but much of it has been dependent on capital and technology imported from First World countries, and on the skills of people originating from those countries. Such a dependence owes much to the legacy of colonial rule. Spain and Portugal discouraged the establishment of industries in their colonies, and apart from the production of some industrial textiles and local handicraft items, manufacturing was largely absent from the continent until the second half of the nineteenth century. It is likely that in 1850 no South American country had even 3 per cent of its GDP resulting from manufacturing,

Fig. 4.1 A tin-concentrating plant at the largest of the tin mines near the town of Potosí in Bolivia. Mining is conducted in hundreds of kilometres of tunnels on fifteen different levels below the buildings in the foreground. The monument in the background marks the top of Cerro Rico, the mountain which has yielded most of the silver (mainly Spanish colonial period) and tin (mainly twentieth century) mined in the region.

and the proportion resulting from true industrial production in factories with ten or more workers was even lower. Since 1850, however, industrialization has occurred in all South American countries, and this process can be broken down into three stages characterized by different forms of dependency. All of the South American countries have embarked on the first stage and moved on to the second, and the two largest, Brazil and Argentina, have entered the third stage.

The first stage of industrialization: processing exports and manufacturing basic consumer goods for local markets

The first stage of industrialization in South America is characterized by the establishment of low-technology industries. Some industries process minerals and farm products for export, and others manufacture simple goods for local consumers.

Processing for export arose in cases where the raw materials were highly perishable or where a major reduction in bulk could be achieved. Raw meat and untanned hides, for example, cannot survive the long sea journey to Europe, so the beef cattle production of the Argentine and Uruguayan Pampas required slaughter-houses and meat-packing, freezing, canning and leather-tanning plants. Similarly, the copper and tin ores produced in the mines of Bolivia (Fig. 4.1) and Chile had to be concentrated, so as to increase the proportion of metal in the ores and to reduce shipping costs. Overland transport was expensive in relation to sea transport, and so exporters close to the coast were at an advantage. The resulting pattern of production and processing industries for export, therefore, showed a high concentration of activity in and around the port-cities.

The growth of cities, the additional incomes generated by export activities, and the spread of new technologies and consumer habits from the First World, all combined to create a larger market for consumer goods in most South American countries. New factories were established in the towns and cities, using fairly simple technologies to produce such basic consumer goods as processed foods, bottled drinks, textiles, clothing, soap and candles. These new urban industries often replaced small-scale traditional production, much of which had been located in rural settlements. As a result, there was not only a growth in manufacturing activity, but also a shift from domestic to factory production, and from rural to urban areas.

Immigrants were important as entrepreneurs, both in export-oriented industries and in those catering for local demands. They imported machinery, trained workers, and established factories in many parts of the continent. The first meat freezing plant in Argentina, for example, was established by an Englishman in 1877. In Brazil, German-owned factories accounted for 90 per cent of the country's textile output in 1916.

In a few cases where local conditions were especially favourable, local consumer industries grew to form the nucleus of more significant industrial expansion. It was shown in Chapter 2 how certain types of primary production for export helped industrialization by generating a basic infrastructure and by providing a large population with sufficient income to purchase industrial goods. Export production in Argentina gave these advantages, and Buenos Aires grew during the late nineteenth and early twentieth centuries into a major industrial centre, well located to serve a large hinterland. São Paulo, with an extensive hinterland opened up for coffee cultivation, had similar advantages. Outside Argentina, Brazil and Chile, however, even the first stage of industrial growth was very small-scale until well into the twentieth century, because the available infrastructure and the size of the domestic market were not capable of supporting more rapid expansion.

The second stage of industrialization: import-substitution

Import-substitution industrialization involves the establishment of new factories to manufacture goods to meet local demands which were previously satisfied by imported goods. The new factories provide industrial jobs for local people. They also reduce the total cost of the country's imports by substituting home-produced for imported goods, so improving the national balance of payments.

The first stimuli to import-substitution industrialization were the disruptions to world trade which resulted from the First World War, the Great Depression (1929–34), and the Second World War. During these periods, the supply of some industrial products was cut off altogether. Some South American countries which exported primary products also suffered severe falls in their exports, because of reduced demand from the industrialized countries of Western Europe and North America. These drops in exports meant that the South American countries could no longer afford to import so many manufactured goods. As a result, particularly in Brazil and Argentina where the domestic markets were largest, new industries were set up to cater for the local demands which were no longer easily satisfied through imports.

Although the Brazilian government offered price guarantees and some transport subsidies to encourage the growth of the iron and steel industry as early as the 1930s, most South American governments did nothing to encourage import-substitution industrialization until after the Second World War. By the early 1950s, virtually all the South American governments were introducing incentives to promote import-substitution industrialization. Such policies were advised by various international organizations, especially the newly-founded United Nations Economic Commission for Latin America (UNECLA). Since the early 1950s the incentives have been increased and they now include a wide variety of price guarantees, transport subsidies, technical assistance, tax concessions, low-interest loans, and machinery grants. Most significant of all, quotas or high tariffs have often been levied on imported finished goods, thus raising the price of these imports and giving the products made within the country a price advantage to gain a foothold in the home market. The first industries to be encouraged have generally been those requiring least capital and least high-level technology, such as textiles, kitchenware and toys. As these industries expanded to supply most of the national demand, and as population increased, a wider range of industries was established. This was particularly true in Brazil and Argentina, where new large-scale industries requiring more capital and high-level technology were founded.

The establishment of the motor vehicle industry in Brazil is an example of a relatively high-technology form of import-substitution industrialization, and an illustration of the continued dependence on the First World. Brazil lacked the technology to create a vehicle industry without outside help, and so foreign companies were encouraged to establish plants in the country. The government offered a number of incentives to foreign investors, as well as guaranteeing the companies protected access to the home market by imposing high tariffs on imported vehicles. The German multinational company, Volkswagen, set up a plant in 1949. During the late 1950s, eleven more foreign vehicle companies came to Brazil, including Ford, General Motors, Mercedes Benz and Toyota. Most established their factories in São Paulo. As a result of this huge foreign investment in Brazil's vehicle industry, very few vehicles had to be imported, and by 1970, 80 per cent of the vehicles on Brazil's roads had been assembled in the country. In addition, most of the parts used in those vehicles had actually been manufactured in Brazil.

Direct government involvement

As well as providing the basic infrastructure needed for industrialization and giving incentives to encourage the foundation of import-substituting industries, South American governments have also taken partial or total ownership of new industries. Sometimes this is done by nationalizing foreign-owned industries, or by taking over firms which have gone bankrupt. Most often, however, government ownership results from the direct investment of government funds in new factories, or the formation of a joint government–private company to establish new industries.

The steel industry is a good example of government involvement in industrial growth. All South American countries with more than 10 million inhabitants have established a steel industry during the import-substitution stage of their industrialization. Any expanding economy requires steel for construction and for making the thousands of steel goods produced by the growing industries. Home production of steel reduces reliance on imports and gives the country a measure of independence, should war break out. Steel is used in most weapons and a home steel industry is often seen as an aid to national military security.

Fig. 4.2 One of the smaller steelworks near the city of Belo Horizonte in the state of Minas Gerais, Brazil. The steelworks manufactures steel ingots from locally mined iron ore.

Alongside its strategic importance, the establishment of a steel industry requires massive investment, because of the complex and costly machinery. The industry therefore is an obvious candidate for state participation.

In Brazil, the government initially encouraged foreign investors to establish steelworks, but became directly involved in the steel industry with the construction of the state-owned Volta Redonda works which was opened in 1946. This was located between the principal markets, São Paulo and Rio de Janeiro, and used iron ore and limestone brought by rail from Minas Gerais, and a mixture of imported and Brazilian coking coal. In the 1950s further steelworks were established by the government, including the large COSIPA works on the coast near São Paulo, and the huge USIMINAS works opened in Minas Gerais in 1956. The latter was established with 59 per cent of the investment coming from the Brazilian government and 40 per cent from Japanese multinational companies. Even in cases where a government apparently provides all the necessary finance, this is usually acquired indirectly from foreign loans. Furthermore, expansion and modernization are also often funded in this way; improvements at the USIMINAS and COSIPA steelworks in 1980, for example, were initiated with an Inter-American Development Bank loan. Foreign dependence is also evident in the use of expensive imported equipment.

Owing largely to government encouragement of the steel industry, Brazil was the world's tenth largest producer of steel by 1980, when it had a total production of 15.3 million tonnes, an amount greater than UK production. Some was exported to the USA and Canada, as well as to various Third World countries. Brazil has more than forty steelworks (Fig. 4.2), although 80 per cent of production comes from the four largest works. Over half of all employees in Brazil's steel industry work for state-owned companies.

The steel industry in other South American countries is on a far smaller scale, and the government role has been even stronger. The Chilean government established the first steel industry in the country in 1950, when the Huachipato plant was opened. Colombia and Peru also established state-owned steelworks in the mid-1950s, with Argentina and

Venezuela following suit a few years later. In these countries, as in Brazil, government control hides high levels of dependency through the use of foreign funds and technology. In addition, in Venezuela the iron-ore supply has been in foreign hands. The national steel industry was established at Ciudad Guyana to use local iron ore which was mined by two American companies.

In some countries of South America the government has played its most active part in the industrial sector of the economy by nationalizing major industries, and such policies have been characteristic of new governments seeking national self-reliance. In Peru the government nationalized the sugar industry in 1969, taking over the major foreign-owned sugar mills and plantations. In the mining industry nationalization has been even more common, and the Peruvian government also operates the major mining companies. Chile nationalized its copper industry in the early 1970s and Venezuela nationalized all oil installations in 1976, a move which affected more than 50 foreign oil companies.

It should be noted that the trend towards increasing government participation has been recently reversed in three countries of South America. This occurred in Chile, Argentina and Uruguay during the mid-to-late 1970s, under the influence of right-wing governments favouring free trade and the private sector. In these countries many government enterprises have been closed down, or sold off to private interests, and some have even been returned to the multinational companies from which they had previously been taken over by more left-wing regimes. In Chile, for example, formerly nationalized banks and industrial companies were sold off after 1973, and only those enterprises regarded as of strategic importance remain in government hands. Many foreign companies have recently established operations in Chile, and in the banking sector, where there had been only one foreign bank in 1973, there were 30 by 1980.

Associated problems

Import-substitution industrialization has quickened the pace of economic growth in South America, at least in the short term. It has not been without disadvantages, however, and some experts argue that it may prove harmful to long-term economic growth and to the welfare of most of the population. Because import-substituting industry has generally been subsidized and protected from foreign competition by quotas or tariffs, production has often been inefficient and the goods have been sold at high prices. This has increased the cost of living and reduced the quality of goods for local consumers, who could obtain cheaper and better imported goods before import-substitution began. The new industries have become heavily reliant on government support to ensure their profitability, and so their managers have often put more effort into influencing the government than into improving industrial efficiency.

Many of the larger industries would probably go out of business if government support were removed. Two such cases are the steel industries in Paz del Rio, Colombia, and in Chimbote, Peru (Fig. 4.3), where it would be cheaper to import the steel than to manufacture it. The Colombian and Peruvian steelworks are too small, technologically outdated, and highly inefficient, to produce steel for sale at competitive prices, without major protection and subsidies from the government. The

Fig. 4.3 The relatively modern steelworks at the town of Chimbote in northern Peru. There is heavy air pollution despite the fact that the plant is working at well below capacity.

high cost of their products puts a considerable burden on the national governments, on taxpayers, and on all industries using steel as a raw material. In turn, these burdens are passed on to the rest of the population through higher prices for locally-manufactured goods containing steel, and through there being less government funds for infrastructure and public services.

The establishment of most import-substituting industries has relied on the import of foreign machinery to manufacture the goods, with an adverse short-term effect on the country's balance of payments. In some cases the cost of machinery imports is as much as ten times the annual cost of importing the goods whose import is being substituted. It can take a full decade before any balance of payments advantage results from import substitution. In many cases also, such industrialization has led to little more than the assembly of imported components in South American countries. Most governments charge tariffs on imported, finished industrial goods, but in order to encourage industrialization in their countries, they do not impose tariffs on the import of manufacturing machinery or components. This policy encourages firms to assemble imported components in the country, but it does not encourage them to manufacture components there. In Colombia's motor vehicle industry, for example, most of the complex components are imported by the multinational companies which own the industry, and only the final assembly is carried out in the country. This enables the companies to take advantage of the Colombian government's tax concessions and protection from competing imports, while at the same time keeping their total investments in Colombia fairly low. The companies employ mainly semi-skilled assembly workers, rather than highly-skilled component makers or technical researchers and design engineers. The benefits of vehicle manufacturing to the Colombian economy are therefore much less than they would be if all stages of the production process were conducted in the country.

Most of the import-substitution industries established in the South American countries show technological and economic dependency on the multinational companies and governments of the First World countries.

Not only do they rely on foreign technology and investment, but also they have to pay for the import of raw materials, components and spares, and for patents and rights of manufacture. In many cases the industries use First World technology which is inappropriate and too sophisticated for South American conditions. Electrical equipment, for example, is frequently made useless in South America by power cuts or voltage fluctuations which blow fuses and damage motors. Simpler equipment based on manual, wind, water or steam power might be more reliable and cheaper, and might also generate more jobs in the industry. In general, however, the appropriate technology is not available because of the lack of research facilities and skills within the country. Further problems may arise when a multinational industrial company threatens to withdraw from the country if the government does not give sufficient concessions or if the workers press for high pay rises. Such withdrawal is particularly likely when nothing more than the final assembly stage of production is conducted in the country, as the multinational company has only made a fairly small investment.

Import-substitution industrialization usually increases dependence on foreign finance in three main ways. First, the funds to establish the new factories often come from abroad, either as loans by foreign banks to local investors or as direct investments by multinational companies. Second, the national governments take foreign loans in order to finance state industries and to provide the basic infrastructure needed by the new industries. Third, the cash incentives and subsidies offered to industries establishing in South American countries are often provided indirectly by foreign loans. These three types of reliance on foreign finance result in large financial outflows, both in the form of interest and repayments on the loans received, and as profits going to the foreign companies which have established factories on the continent.

The third stage of industrialization: export promotion and the manufacture of capital goods

The third stage of industrialization is often known as 'general industrialization' because it implies the expansion of all types of industries, and not just export-processing or the manufacture of consumer goods. In particular, it involves the establishment of industries to manufacture capital goods such as cranes, turbines and factory machinery, and the expansion of many industries selling goods abroad as well as to the domestic market. The only South American country which has fully entered this stage is Brazil, although Argentina also has some of the characteristics of general industrialization.

During the 1950s Brazil was a good example of the advantages of import-substitution industrialization, in encouraging economic growth, and in supplying national consumer demands. By the early 1960s, however, the rate of industrial expansion was slowing down. The country entered a period of economic and political crisis leading to the revolution of 1964, when a right-wing military government took power. This new government laid the economic and political foundations for a new 'development model' which continued into the 1980s. While most other South American governments in the early 1960s were considering land reform as a means of overcoming their economic and political problems (see Chapter 3), the new Brazilian government opted wholeheartedly for general industrialization. This involved the introduction of new high-technology industries, the promotion of industrial exports, and the manufacture of a wide range of capital goods. Brazil launched into a period of rapid industrialization and economic growth between 1968 and 1973, the so-called 'economic miracle'.

The Brazilian government's policies to encourage general industrialization have included heavy state investments in key industries, and many concessions to multinational companies willing to invest in the country. The petrochemical industry, for example, has been expanded rapidly under a combination of government and multinational ownership, with four of the ten largest concerns belonging to government corporations and a further four to multinationals. Foreign companies dominate most of the more dynamic industries in Brazil, including engineering and the manufacture of motor vehicles, electrical and pharmaceutical goods. Some multinational companies have reinvested their profits in expanding their industries, or in establishing agribusinesses and buying up large areas of land in Brazil. Most of them, however, have sent the profits made in Brazil to the companies' countries of origin. Even in those companies which are largely or entirely Brazilian-owned, there is usually a heavy reliance on foreign technology. For multinational companies it can be good business to sell equipment to Brazilian firms, but it is rarely profitable to sell the information on how to make such equipment, or the expertise to enable Brazilian firms to do all their own research and design work.

Despite Brazil's massive foreign debt, the largest in the Third World, its reliance on multinational companies, and its technological dependency, many politicians and industrialists feel that the other South American countries should follow Brazil's example and start general industrialization. With the possible exception of Argentina, however, these countries have little short-term chance of success. The most obvious problem is the small size of their domestic markets. Their total populations are too small (see Table 4.1 page 72), and on average too poor, for them to build up large-scale industries before trying to sell their products abroad. In addition, most countries lack the necessary infrastructure for major industrial expansion and several countries, particularly Bolivia, also lack the political stability necessary to carry out the required policies.

Industrial concentration

In the first stage of industrialization, new industries were fairly widely spread across South America. Export-processing factories were located in many mining areas, port-cities and coastal agricultural regions; and simple industries supplying a local market were located in most of the main towns and cities. Even in this first stage, there were signs of industrial concentration around the River Plate estuary in Argentina and Uruguay, and in South-East Brazil, but there were no major clusters of industry in specific cities. Industrialization was still not a major factor in the growth of the main cities. The industries established during this stage were merely supporting activities for export-oriented farming and mining, or supplying urban centres whose economies were based on trade, administration and handicrafts.

Fig. 4.4 A central district in the city of Rio de Janeiro, Brazil. Industries characteristic of the first and second stages of industrialization are clustered together in dilapidated buildings. The newer apartment and office blocks to the rear are part of the expanding central business district of the city, and there are now pressures for the demolition of the factories to make way for additional tower blocks.

In the second stage of industrialization, major concentrations of industrial activity have begun to emerge in specific cities of South America (Fig. 4.4). Furthermore, it is those regions with most second-stage industrialization, South-East Brazil and the Buenos Aires Metropolitan Region in Argentina, which have gone into the third stage of industrialization. In turn, the industries established in this third stage have contributed to further concentration in those same regions, widening the inequalities in average per capita incomes and total wealth between those regions and the rest of the continent.

The majority of modern industries in the second and third stages of industrialization operate most efficiently in large factories. This is because of internal economies of scale. The larger the output from a factory, the lower the average costs of production. The products are then cheaper and so can compete successfully with those of rival manufacturers. As a result, industrialists usually choose locations where conditions are suitable for a large factory. They need sufficient raw materials, land and labour, and often most important of all, easy access to a large market.

In general, the most profitable locations for the industries established in the second and third stages of industrialization lie in the main cities and most densely populated regions of South America. These areas usually have relatively good infrastructure and labour supplies, as well as large concentrations of potential customers for the industrial products. Ever since the early colonial period in South America, people living in the cities have on average been far wealthier than those in the rural areas. This increases the attractiveness of the cities as locations for industries producing consumer goods, because consumer demand is so heavily concentrated there.

The concentration of new industries in and around the major cities is further encouraged because many industries operate more cheaply and easily if they are located close to other industries. These advantages of concentration are called agglomeration economies. For example, industries clustered together can share specialized transport facilities such as a rail freight terminal, and they can also share skilled service engineers to mend their machinery. Linkages between industries are also easier where there is agglomeration, as components made in one factory are easily passed to another, for use in the assembly of vehicles or machinery. These agglomeration economies have a particularly strong influence on the location decisions of foreign companies, whose representatives may have little or no knowledge of the country outside its major city. Moreover, as South American governments increase their involvement in the industrial sector through subsidies, incentives, controls and joint government–private ownership, industrial companies are strongly attracted to the cities where key government agencies are located. This again favours location in the major cities and particularly the capital city, as it is there that influential politicians and administrators can be contacted most easily.

Industrialization has contributed to the growth of the main cities of the continent through a process known as 'circular and cumulative causation', which can be explained as follows. The first industries producing consumer goods were located close to the market, in or around the main existing cities. These industries generated more jobs, more income for workers and the greater availability of consumer goods in those cities and their surrounding areas. This extra prosperity provided more local capital for investment and increased local consumer demand, and so attracted new firms to establish factories in the same cities. The labour requirements of the new industries, combined with the extra jobs available in the cities for traders, transporters, construction workers and domestic servants, attracted migrants from the surrounding countryside and from other regions. This in-migration increased the size of the local market for consumer goods as well as the available labour supply, attracting further industries to locate in the cities. In turn, these further industries led to more agglomeration economies, more demand for labour, and more in-migration, so the cities continued increasing in size.

On a continental scale as well as a national scale, the concentration of industry into the major cities is such that one or several cities usually constitute a core of prosperous economic activity, which contrasts markedly with the poverty of the periphery (Fig. 4.5). In Argentina, Buenos Aires has been a core area of industrial concentration for many decades. The city, with over 10 million inhabitants, has a population larger than that of any of the six smallest countries in South America. Because of the greater purchasing power, the relatively wealthy population of Buenos Aires provides a far larger market for industrial goods than its size alone might indicate. The same comments apply to the large concentration of population and industry in and around São Paulo. In 1985 there were over 15 million people in Greater São Paulo, and the core-periphery phenomenon is even more pronounced in Brazil than in Argentina. The South-East region, including São Paulo, Rio de Janeiro and Belo Horizonte, is developing into the core region of the whole continent. In 1970, 70 per cent of industrial employment in Brazil was found in this region. The region holds the majority of Brazil's steelworks, petrochemical plants and industries producing consumer goods. São Paulo and its satellite towns constitute the nucleus, with over one-third of the country's industrial employment. Many of Brazil's most dynamic industries are clustered here, and the nucleus holds over half of the country's employment in electrical and plastics industries. Most of the multinational vehicle manufacturers operate in Greater São Paulo.

Fig. 4.5 The major core areas of South America.

multinational vehicle manufacturers operate in Greater São Paulo.

The development of Brazil's core industrial area has its origins in the nineteenth century. The excellent infrastructure established in the early coffee era provided a firm basis for the growth of industry. Beginning with textiles and food-processing industries, São Paulo became the major centre for the manufacture of clothing and later artificial fibres, and also chemicals. The expansion and wealth of the city makes it a large market for consumer goods, and the excellent transport links give easy access to an even wider national and international market.

In all the countries of South America, except Argentina, the concentration of manufacturing industry into the major cities became more pronounced between 1930 and 1970. The cities which already have the most wealth are made even wealthier by this process of concentration. The highest wages and the largest tax revenues to local and national governments are found in the major cities with most industry. These wages and taxes, combined with the concentration of political and economic power in the cities, have stimulated large investments in housing, infrastructure, (Figs. 4.6 and 4.7), and public services. In turn, these wages, taxes and local investments have widened the spatial inequalities in incomes, wealth and social provision between the cities and the peripheral regions of the country.

Policies to encourage industrial dispersal

South American governments have become increasingly aware of the growing problem of spatial inequalities between core and peripheral regions, and particularly between the major cities of the core regions and the rural areas on the periphery. Political pressures from interest groups on the periphery have combined with growing concern about congestion and pollution in the major cities, to persuade governments to take steps to encourage the dispersal of industries.

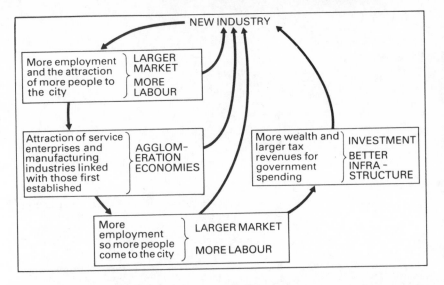

Fig. 4.6 The process of circular and cumulative causation as applied to industrialization and urbanization.

NEW INDUSTRY

More employment and the attraction of more people to the city } LARGER MARKET MORE LABOUR

Attraction of service enterprises and manufacturing industries linked with those first established } AGGLOM-ERATION ECONOMIES

More wealth and larger tax revenues for government spending } INVESTMENT BETTER INFRA-STRUCTURE

More employment so more people come to the city } LARGER MARKET MORE LABOUR

Fig. 4.7 Construction of the giant Itaipu hydroelectric dam on the Paraná river. This is the world's largest hydro-electric power project, and this photograph taken in 1980, shows only about a tenth of the total construction works. Since 1983, electricity has gone by high-voltage transmission lines to supply Greater São Paulo.

These policies, have taken two main forms: first, offering financial incentives to industries establishing in a peripheral region, and second, building up selected new or existing towns in peripheral regions as industrial growth centres for the country. Brazil is the most important example of the first, where incentives are offered to firms setting up in the North-East. Since the establishment of a special North-East development agency in 1959, Brazilian firms have been able to write off half their tax dues as investment capital for the North-East. By the end of 1970, about 750 industrial projects had taken this financial support, many in order to expand their existing factories. Overall, however, the impact on industrial growth in the region has been limited. The second, growth centre, approach is best illustrated by the Venezuelan policy to generate industrial growth at Ciudad Guayana. In 1961 the city was founded at the confluence of the rivers Orinoco and Caroni, where an existing town of nearly 50,000 people had grown up alongside the iron ore mines, a steel mill and hydroelectric power station (Fig. 4.8). Ciudad Guayana was planned as a centre for large-scale manufacturing industry and as a focal

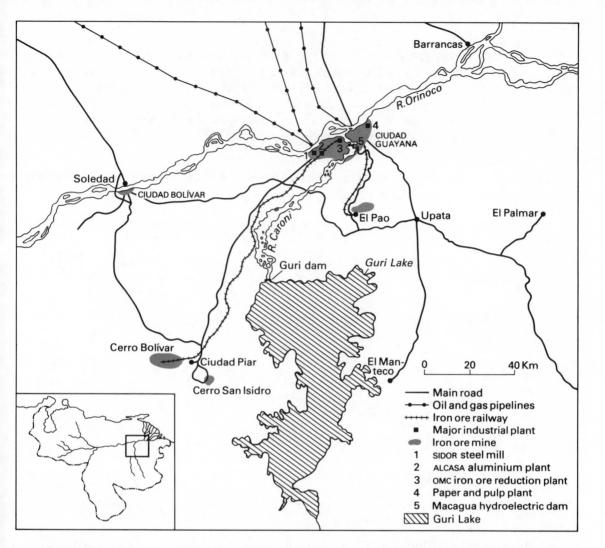

Fig. 4.8 Industrial activities in Ciudad Guayana and vicinity. Several of Venezuela's principal oilfields and the main zone of potentially-exploitable extra heavy crude oil reserves (the Orinoco oil belt) are located just to the north and north-west of the area shown on this map. Updated from W. Karlsson, *Manufacturing in Venezuela: Studies on development and location*, Institute of Latin American Studies, Stockholm (1975).

Map legend:
— Main road
• Oil and gas pipelines
++++ Iron ore railway
■ Major industrial plant
Iron ore mine
1 SIDOR steel mill
2 ALCASA aluminium plant
3 OMC iron ore reduction plant
4 Paper and pulp plant
5 Macagua hydroelectric dam
Guri Lake

point for the economic development of eastern Venezuela. The Ciudad Guayana scheme has been moderately successful in establishing a major urban and industrial centre in east-central Venezuela, but few South American governments could afford or manage such a large and costly project.

Whether through regional incentives as in Brazil, or the establishment of new cities in peripheral regions as in Venezuela, the policies pursued by most governments to encourage dispersal have achieved little. Foreign companies in particular are not prepared to accept anything but the economically optimum location, which is almost always in or near a major city. Both multinational and domestic companies are mainly concerned to maximize their profits. They are unlikely to go to the poorer regions unless very strong incentives are offered by government, or unless major natural resources are discovered which offer scope for extraction and processing of raw materials.

The pros and cons of industrialization

Industrial expansion has generated considerable economic growth in certain countries and regions of South America. In most countries, industry has been the fastest expanding sector of the economy. In Brazil,

71

during the 1968–1973 period of the 'economic miracle', there was an average GDP growth of 9 per cent per annum, with an average growth in the industrial sector of 13 per cent per annum. By the late 1970s manufactured goods accounted for over half of Brazil's exports, and the economy became much less reliant on imports of consumer goods or the export of food and raw materials.

Table 4.1   The contribution of manufacturing industry to GDP, and employment by country, 1985

Country	Value added to GDP by manufacturing in 1985 (millions of 1986 US$)	Manufacturing as % of GDP in 1985	% of economically active population in manu-facturing 1980	Total population (millions) 1985
Brazil	81,181	25.2	27	135.6
Argentina	13,939	20.1	34	30.5
Venezuela	9,828	20.5	28	17.3
Colombia	7,798	21.2	24	28.4
Chile	5,469	20.4	25	12.1
Peru	5,020	21.6	18	18.6
Ecuador	2,172	17.3	20	9.4
Uruguay	1,319	17.5	29	3.0
Paraguay	1,155	16.6	21	3.7
Bolivia	619	9.8	20	6.4
Suriname	149	13.4	—	0.4
Guyana	62	10.1	—	0.8

Source: Inter-American Development Bank, *1987 Report*; World Bank, *World Development Report 1987*.

Outside Brazil and Argentina the level of industrialization is very low. Industry generally contributes less than a quarter of GDP (Table 4.1) and employs a small proportion of the total labour force, for example about 11 per cent in Colombia, and only 3 per cent in Bolivia. The fact that most of the discussion in this chapter focuses on Brazil simply reflects Brazil's position as the only South American country where industrial production has reached significant proportions in relation to total world output. In Brazil the value of industrial production in 1985 was six times greater than in Argentina alone, and more than twice that of all world, and since then it has consistently been one of the largest industrial producers and exporters of the Third World. Industrial growth in the smaller South American countries has been stifled by competition from the First World countries, from newly-industrializing countries in Asia, such as Singapore, Taiwan and South Korea, and from Brazil and Argentina.

The attempts to establish international groupings of South American countries as free-trade areas along the lines of the European Economic Community, have done little to stave off the flow of industrial goods from outside the continent. Some have claimed that such groupings have merely favoured the interests of North American, European and Japanese multinationals willing to establish South American assembly plants, and of Brazilian exporters seeking to expand their markets. In 1960, the Latin American Free Trade Association (LAFTA), was formed with the aim of international economic integration as a way towards industrial growth. By reducing some tariff barriers between member countries, which comprise almost all South American countries and Mexico, LAFTA helped to stimulate the industrialization of Brazil, Mexico and Argentina, but did little to assist the industrialization of the other countries. The opportunities provided for international trade were captured by the larger manufacturers who could produce goods most cheaply. These manufacturers were located in the most highly industrialized countries, and particularly in the core regions of those countries. LAFTA, therefore, merely strengthened the process of circular and cumulative causation, whereby the more industrialized countries and regions maintained and even increased their lead over the less industrialized countries and regions. The disadvantages of LAFTA for the smaller and less industrialized countries were a major factor behind the creation of the Andean Pact in 1969, an association which deliberately excluded the more industrialized countries of Latin America. Although this smaller organization, made up of Bolivia, Colombia, Ecuador, Peru and Venezuela, had some initial success, it has subsequently achieved little. There has been disagreement about a common external tariff and key industrial programmes, and relations between member countries have been hindered by a series of border disputes.

In all countries of South America, industry has the potential to yield tax revenues which can provide the government with the resources to improve the welfare of the population. However, tax revenues are often quite small because of the tax exemptions granted as incentives to persuade industrialists to establish plants, and because the industrialists put pressure on the government to keep taxation very low. A further factor reducing the amount of tax revenue from industry is that the multinational companies are skilled at adjusting their accounts to shift activities and prices between countries in such a way as to minimize their tax payments. Even the tax that is collected is not often spent on improving the welfare of the population as a whole. Instead, most of it is usually spent on increasing the power of the government by creating jobs for political supporters, by investing in prestige projects, and by strengthening the armed forces.

The failure to yield large tax revenues to improve the welfare of the population is just one of the many problems of South American industrialization. It has also failed to reduce unemployment on any scale, mainly because population expansion has continued while industrial growth has involved new manufacturing plants which often employ few people. Indeed, some new industries have even reduced employment by installing mechanized production and so destroying the livelihood of hundreds or thousands of artisans who cannot compete with the new technology. New industries have replaced traditional handicrafts, and shoes, for example, once hand-made in many small workshops are now mainly produced in highly-mechanized factories. Industrialization has failed to reduce social inequalities. The poorest people in Brazil were considered relatively worse off by the late 1970s than they had been in the 1960s, although many investors, managers and technicians were

Fig. 4.9 The cement factory located beside a tidal creek on the western edge of the city of Guayaquil, Ecuador. Dust and smoke from the factory pollutes the environment over a large area of poor housing called the suburbio in the western half of the city.

much better off. Just as industrialization has not helped the poorest people, neither has it helped the poor, peripheral regions. Instead, industrialization has been concentrated in core areas. The rich areas have become even richer and so the differences in wealth between the rich and poor areas have become even greater.

Industrialization can also be considered undesirable because of its effects on health, agriculture and the environment. The large-scale manufacture of alcoholic drinks and cigarettes, for example, has undoubtedly generated health problems. Government policies to encourage industrialization have often been pursued to the detriment of the agricultural sector, where government investments and incentives to increase production have generally been small in relation to the size and importance of the sector. Furthermore, in their enthusiasm to promote industrialization, governments have often paid scant attention to environmental controls, so that large-scale pollution has sometimes been an unfortunate side-effect of industrialization (Figs. 4.9 and 4.3). Foreign companies have been only too glad to establish highly polluting industries in South American countries where the expensive anti-pollution measures demanded in most First World countries are not required.

Some of the disadvantages of industrialization are associated with foreign domination in the industrial sector. Indeed, many would argue that the long-term economic growth and welfare of South American countries would be helped if multinational companies played a lesser role in industrial expansion. Foreign companies are likely to locate and operate with foreign rather than national priorities in mind, and many intend to take any profits they make out of South America altogether. It can be argued, therefore, that the South American countries gain very little from such investments, apart from short-term boosts to their economic growth rates. Moreover, the multinationals may reduce the opportunities for local industrial companies in two ways: first, by attracting government support, private investment and skilled personnel which might otherwise have gone to the local companies; and second, because their products sell much better than those of the local companies, because of more effective advertising and the prestige of international

Fig. 4.10 This simple brick-making machine is an example of appropriate technology, suitable for rural areas and remote towns where industrially-produced bricks are expensive and factory production is not worthwhile. The machine, used by a co-operative group with support from Oxfam, cost about £250 in 1981. It can be operated by two persons and can produce about 120 bricks per hour.

brand names. Most seriously of all, the heavy reliance of most industry on the multinational companies exposes the South American governments to the risk of economic blackmail by the multinationals, and their First World (home) governments. When South American governments have adopted policies against the interests of some multinationals, as in Chile between 1970 and 1973 and in Peru between 1969 and 1975, many multinationals have exerted pressure to cut off trade, investment and economic aid. In such cases multinational companies have helped to cause an economic crisis in a South American country, and sometimes they have even tried to promote the overthrow of the government. Dependence on multinational companies, therefore, can limit the range of policies which South American governments can adopt, and it can lead to outside intervention in the internal affairs of their countries.

Industrialization can contribute to the reduction of inequalities and the provision of basic needs in South America, if a careful balance is struck between concerns for economic growth, efficient production, and social objectives. With this in mind, industries could be fostered to produce goods at low prices for the mass of the population. Industry could also be geared to generate income and employment for as many people as possible. This objective may involve choosing intermediate technology, which is simpler and more labour-intensive than the complex, capital-intensive technology so often adopted (Fig. 4.10). While industrialization remains economically and technologically dependent on the multinational companies and governments of the First World countries, however, there is little hope of such policies being put into effect. If there are no major political and social upheavals in South America, dependency is likely to remain a feature of their economies and particularly of their industrialization. As there seems little prospect of fundamental upheavals in the late 1980s and 1990s, the main arguments about industrialization tend to focus on three issues. First, whether to increase, hold constant or reduce government investments in industry relative to such other sectors as agriculture and education. Second, how much subsidy, incentive or protection from foreign competition, governments should give to industries in their countries. Third, how dependence on foreign capital and technology might be changed to allow a build-up of local capital and technical skills, and to encourage industrial growth based on national, rather than foreign, resources. Even among industrialists and economic policymakers there are great differences of opinion on each issue, and the various governments in South America follow widely differing policies.

5 Urban expansion

South America has seen a huge growth in the size and number of its cities, and a major expansion in its urban population over the past thirty years. In 1960, eight out of twelve countries in the continent had the majority of their populations living in rural areas (Table 5.1). By 1985, only three countries were left in this position, and by 1980 there were at least 29 cities with populations over $^1/_2$ million (Fig. 5.1). Four countries now have over 80 per cent of their populations living in towns and cities, and only three of the smaller and poorer countries, Bolivia, Guyana and Paraguay, still have less than half their populations defined as urban.

The rapid urban population growth in South America has taken place at a time of rapid national population growth. Chapter 2 described how the latter has been due to high birth rates and falling death rates in both urban and rural areas. However, because of migration from rural to urban areas, most of the population increase since 1950 has been in the cities and towns. In the period 1960–1979, for example, Brazil's population increased by 49 million, but of that increase 43 million was in the cities and towns. Outside the most urbanized countries of South America, average urban population growth rates were between 3.5 and 4.5 per cent per annum during the 1970s (Table 5.1). Lima, with a

Table 5.1 The percentage of the population living in urban areas by country 1960–1985

Country (in order of % population urban in 1985)	Urban[a] population as % of total population 1960	1985	1985 per capita GNP US$	Average annual % growth rate of urban population 1970–80	% of urban population in largest city 1980
MOST URBANIZED					
Uruguay	80	85	1,650	0.7	52
Venezuela	67	85	3,080	4.2	26
Argentina	74	84	2,130	1.8	45
Chile	68	83	1,430	2.4	44
INTERMEDIATE					
Brazil	46	73	1,640	4.3	15
Peru	46	68	1,010	4.4	39
Colombia	48	67	1,320	3.9	26
Suriname	—	58	2,580	—	—
LEAST URBANIZED					
Ecuador	34	52	1,160	4.5	29
Bolivia	24	44	470	4.3	44
Paraguay	36	41	860	3.5	44
Guyana	20	31	500	—	—

[a.] Using national definitions of urban

Sources: Inter-American Development Bank, *1979 Report;* World Bank, *World Development Report 1980, 1987.*

77

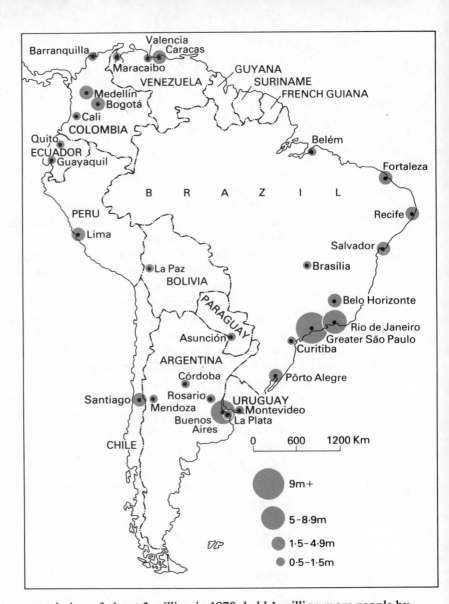

Fig. 5.1 Cities of over half a million population in 1980.

9m+

5–8·9m

1·5–4·9m

0·5–1·5m

population of about 3 million in 1970, held 1 million more people by 1980. São Paulo grew from 5 million in 1965 to over 8 million in 1980. If the towns surrounding São Paulo are included because they now form part of a continuous urban area, by 1985 Greater São Paulo was estimated to have 15 million inhabitants. This is the largest conurbation in the continent.

The process of urbanization has been very pronounced in South America since 1950. Urbanization means that the urban proportion of the national population is growing, and that more and more people are living in towns and cities. Urbanization and rapid city growth are caused by rural–urban migration and by a high rate of natural increase. The migration involves millions of people moving from the countryside and regional towns to the cities. Country-folk will often move first to a town and then to a city, or have several trial periods of working in a city before making a final move. Thus the majority of migrants to the city usually have some experience of urban life before they settle there on a permanent basis. Most migrants are young and single or recently married, so that most of their children are born in the city, which obviously adds to

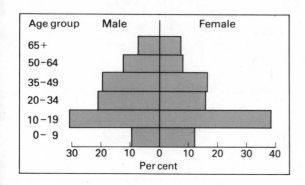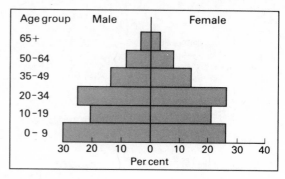

Fig. 5.2 Age distribution of immigrants in Bogotá, 1970−75. Source of data: International Labour Office, *Bogotá: Urban development and employment*, ILO, Geneva, 1978.

Fig. 5.3 Age distribution of total population, Bogotá, 1975. Source: As Fig. 5.2.

the urban birth rate. The high rate of natural increase common in South American cities is, therefore, mainly caused by the high rate of in-migration of young adults, and by the resulting high proportion of young adults in the population (Figs. 5.2 and 5.3).

Primacy

Urbanization in South America has usually involved the biggest city in each country growing far larger than the other cities. In many countries around the world, there is a regular distribution of cities which can be described by the rank−size rule. That is, the largest city is roughly double the size of the second largest, treble the size of the third largest city and so on (Fig. 5.4 and Table 5.2). This rank−size distribution is often considered to be desirable and normal. In all countries of South America,

Table 5.2   The rank−size rule and the cities of selected countries (the ratio of the population of the next four largest cities to the population of the largest city).

Country (year)	Rank 1	Rank 2	Rank 3	Rank 4	Rank 5
Rank−size rule	1.00	0.50	0.33	0.25	0.20
Argentina (1975)	1.00	0.10	0.09	0.06	0.06
Brazil (1980)	1.00	0.71	0.20	0.18	0.18
Chile (1970)	1.00	0.17	0.16	0.04	0.04
Peru (1972)	1.00	0.09	0.07	0.06	0.05
Venezuela (1970)	1.00	0.33	0.19	0.18	0.16

Sources: *Statistical Abstract of Latin America*, 20 (1980); International Labour Office, *Bogotá: Urban Development and Employment*, ILO, Geneva (1978); *Latin America Regional Reports: Brazil*, 3 July 1981.

except Brazil, Colombia and Ecuador, the largest city is far more than twice as large as any other city, and there is a wide gap in size and importance between the major city and other cities. This is described as primacy (Fig. 5.4). Instead of a rank−size distribution of cities, the distribution is very top heavy, and is often seen as inappropriate and abnormal. Primacy probably has its origins in the colonial era, when the links between each administrative region and Spain or Portugal were channelled through only one city. The growth of this one city became even more significant when industrialization occurred. In recent decades, primacy has continued because the largest cities have been growing as fast as, or faster than, most of the smaller cities.

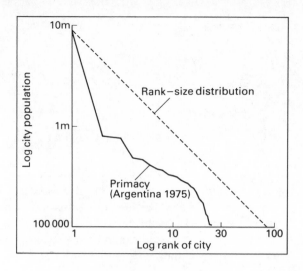

Fig. 5.4 The size distribution of cities:
a. The rank – size distribution
b. Primacy: the case of Argentina in 1975. Source of data: 1975 Argentine Population Census.

Urban growth and inequality

The rapid growth of cities in the South American countries has been associated with growing differences in wealth between different areas. These spatial inequalities are not only in total wealth, but also average per capita wealth.

Urbanization and wealth

The inequalities between countries can be measured by per capita GDP or per capita GNP as defined in Chapter 1. Table 5.1 shows how the differences in per capita GNP are linked with the proportion of the national population which lives in towns and cities. All countries with more than 2,000 US dollars per capita GNP in 1985 had at least 58 per cent of their population defined as urban. The poorest countries of South America, those with less than 1,000 US dollars per capita GNP, had less than half of their populations defined as urban. Major inequalities in wealth between countries also explain most international migration, for example the flow of Colombians into Venezuela and the flow of Bolivians into Argentina seeking better-paid jobs in the wealthier country.

The association between cities and wealth can also be seen within countries. The wealthiest region is normally the region with the largest city or cities (Fig. 5.5). The only exception to this rule is in Bolivia where the population of the region of Santa Cruz, the second city, is on average wealthier than that of the region around La Paz, the capital. The Santa Cruz region has benefited from the illegal cocaine trade and from its rich resources, which include oil, natural gas and fertile farming land. In Brazil the wealthy state of São Paulo, with its large urban population, has average per capita incomes which are more than twice those in the poor North-East region of the country. Differences in wealth are, of course, linked with other inequalities. People in poorer areas are less likely to have learnt to read and write, and they are more likely to die young. In 1970 people on average lived until they were 58 years old in São Paulo state, but only 44 years in North-East Brazil.

On a different scale, the inequality between city and countryside is marked in all countries of South America. Information for Brazil shows

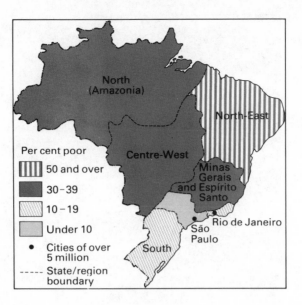

Fig. 5.5 The regional distribution of poverty in Brazil 1974/75. The number of families with an income of less than two minimum wages is expressed as a percentage of the total families in the region. Source: *World Bank Staff Working Paper* No 356, 1979.

that the average urban per capita income in the 1970s was about 2½ times more than the average rural per capita income. Data for the North-East of Brazil show even wider variations in wealth depending on where a family lives within the region. In 1974/75 an index of average family income was 100 in the countryside of the North-East, 200 in the towns, 300 in the city of Fortaleza, and 590 in the city of Salvador.

Rural–urban migration

The inequality between city and countryside is the major reason for the rural–urban migration which has helped to cause the rapid urban growth. In the countryside, average incomes are low because agricultural wages are poor, and because landholdings are often so small that farmers earn very little. Moreover, incomes are uncertain because they are generally tied to the success of the harvest. A harvest failure can mean starvation. Rural living conditions are miserable because electricity and piped drinking water are usually unavailable, and doctors and schools are few. Living conditions are often not much better in the rural villages and market towns. People from the countryside and towns are attracted to the cities by the chance of a job, and because cities have the best schools, the best hospitals, and the best recreational facilities, such as cinemas and football stadiums. People move because they think that they will be better off and happier in the cities.

The distribution of income

Information on average per capita incomes shows only the amount of income received in a country or area in relation to the number of people, without showing anything about the way the money is distributed within that country or area. In all parts of South America there is a vast contrast between the wealth of the relatively few rich people and the poverty of the many poor. Recent studies of incomes in Brazil, for example, have shown how small a share of the total family income or wealth is taken by the poorest 40 per cent of the population. In 1960, the poorest 40 per cent

Fig. 5.6 Rich housing in the city of Cali, Colombia. The large houses surrounded by private gardens lie at the foot of the hill on the west side of the city.

Fig. 5.7 Lower middle-income housing in Cali. Here the houses are soundly built of brick and concrete, but have only one storey. The streets are generally left unpaved.

had only a 9.8 per cent share of the total family income, a share which fell to 8.4 per cent in 1970, and 7.8 per cent in 1976. Meanwhile, the share of the richest 10 per cent of the population rose slightly from 50.0 per cent in 1960 to 51.5 per cent in 1970, and to 51.9 per cent in 1974/75. The data not only show the sharp inequalities between rich and poor, but also suggest that the inequality has increased during the 1960s and 1970s, which included a period of rapid economic growth. This growth has not benefited the poor in Brazil to any great extent; for many of the poorest people, it may actually have worsened their situation.

The highly unequal spread of income is an important feature of all South American countries. It makes them very different to most First World countries, where inequalities are less extreme and the richest 10 per cent usually has only about a 25 per cent share of the total family income. Within South American cities themselves, the inequality between rich and poor is immediately visible from the contrasting appearance of the different neighbourhoods (Figs. 5.6–5.9). Large houses with servants'

Fig. 5.8 Poor housing on the north-eastern edge of Cali. This shanty-town occupies a field which was taken over in an organized invasion five months before this photograph was taken. Some plank-walled and tile-roofed houses are already established, and some householders have already built themselves pit latrines. Other houses are still only in the first stage of construction.

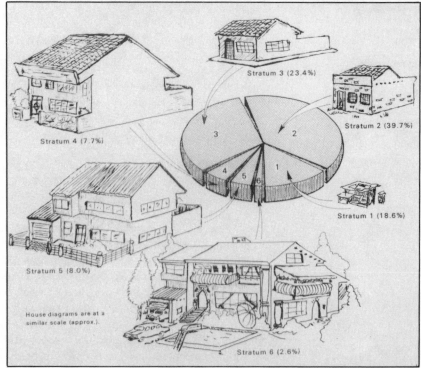

Fig. 5.9 The physical appearance, size and numerical significance of the typical houses in the six officially defined socio-economic strata in Cali in 1976. All houses are drawn to the same scale. The percentages and also the proportions of the divided 'pie' indicate the proportions of total population in each stratum.

quarters, private swimming pools and several garages provide luxury homes for the rich. The poor household may only have a shack, with no water tap, toilet or electricity.

The urban economy: the two circuits

The economy of a city in South America, although fairly similar to that of most cities in Africa or Asia, is very different from that of a West European or North American city. Most recent studies of South American cities have described the urban economy as consisting of two different, but interlinked, sectors, the one dominant and the other

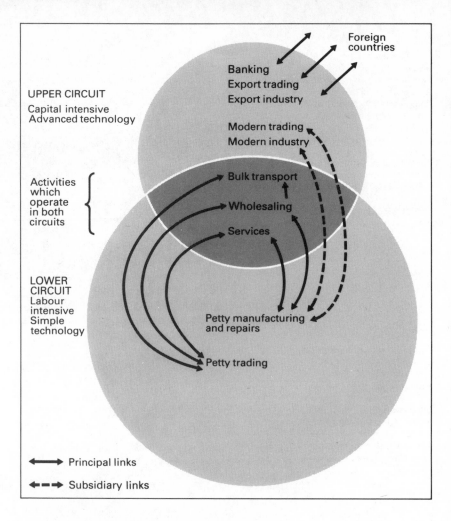

Fig. 5.10 Relations between the upper and lower circuits of the urban economy. After M. Santos, *The Shared Space,* Methuen (1979).

subordinate. The two sectors have been described by Milton Santos as the upper and lower circuits. Using Santos's terms, Fig. 5.10 shows the structure of the typical South American city economy.

The upper circuit of the economy includes banking, export trade and also wholesaling, bulk transport and services. This part of the economy is like that of cities in the First World. These activities use advanced technology, and require a large investment of money before they start operating. They use relatively little labour. Multinational companies are strongly represented in the upper circuit, operating branch factories and having partial control of many local firms. Most people working in the upper circuit have regular employment with wages, some degree of job security, and access to social security. By the standards of their countries, these people are around the middle of the social scale. They may not be very wealthy or privileged, but they do not suffer from the extremes of poverty and deprivation experienced by the poorest people.

The lower circuit of the urban economy is associated with poverty because it provides most of the jobs which are available to the urban poor, and it produces many of the goods and services that the poor can afford. It comprises a huge variety of small-scale activities, including petty manufacturing, petty trading, and personal services. Technology is simple and the work is labour-intensive rather than relying on complex machinery. The equipment used is usually of poor quality and often out of date. Most equipment and materials are used again and again so that little is wasted. Old rubber tyres, for example, are cut into sandals, and scrap pieces of wood are made into chairs. Most people seem to work on their own or as part of a family enterprise, but in reality many are dependent on others, such as wholesalers and moneylenders, for their work. Earnings are irregular and unpredictable. Working contacts tend to be confined to the city itself, in contrast to the national and international links of the upper-circuit activities. The banks are rarely used in the lower circuit, and business agreements, such as exist, tend to be informal and between individuals (see Table 5.3).

Table 5.3   The characteristics of the two circuits of the urban economy

	Upper circuit	Lower circuit
Technology	capital-intensive	labour-intensive
Organization	bureaucratic	primitive
Capital	abundant	limited
Labour	limited	abundant
Regular wages	prevalent	exceptional
Inventories	large quantities, and/or high quality	small quantities, poor quality
Prices	generally fixed	negotiable between buyer and seller (haggling)
Credit	from banks, institutional	personal, non-institutional
Profit margin	small per unit, but large turnover	large per unit, but small turnover
Relations with customers	impersonal and/or on paper	direct, personal
Fixed costs	substantial	negligible
Advertisement	necessary	none
Re-use of goods	none (waste)	frequent
Overhead capital	essential	not essential
Government aid	extensive	none or almost none
Direct dependence on foreign countries	great, externally orientated	small or none

Source: Milton Santos, *The Shared Space,* Methuen, London (1979).

The two circuits are closely linked, with the lower generally being dependent on the upper. Some activities such as wholesaling and cargo transport perform intermediary roles linking the two circuits. Wholesalers, for example, often distribute goods made by upper-circuit manufacturers to lower-circuit petty traders who sell from street or market stalls or from small shops.

Until the 1970s little was known about activities in the lower circuit, and views still differ about the circuit's role in the city economy. Compared with the upper circuit, its productivity, in terms of the value of goods produced and the quantity of labour used, is extremely low. However, minimal amounts of capital, whether in the form of money or equipment, are often used very efficiently in the lower-circuit. Also, the labour used is generally very cheap because advantage is taken of child workers, old and handicapped people, and family labour. These people would probably find no work in the upper circuit, or would legally be prevented from working anyway. The lower circuit plays a major role in holding down the cost of living for both rich and poor people in the city, because it provides an abundance of cheap, labour-intensive goods and services. Thousands of people seeking work can be absorbed in the lower circuit, but the kinds of work that most of those people find do not lift them out of their poverty. Thus, by providing incomes and by reducing the cost of living, the lower circuit enables the poor to survive. However, it offers few opportunities for the poor to gain wealth. The profits made in the lower circuit usually pass through the hands of people like wholesalers and moneylenders, and go into the upper circuit which dominates the city economy.

The struggle for employment

The vast growth of city population has increased the struggle for employment. When urbanization was particularly rapid in nineteenth-century Western Europe and North America, it was associated with fast industrial growth. Most people who moved to the cities were able to take jobs in the new factories. In South America industrial growth has been slow compared with urban growth. The lack of factory jobs is one of the causes of the large service sector of the economy. This sector includes all those activities which do not produce goods but simply provide services, for example: trading, transport, catering, domestic service, administration, education and health care. In the city of Cali, Colombia, statistics for 1977 show that 64 per cent of the working population was in the service sector, while only 27 per cent was engaged in manufacturing. In other South American cities the picture is similar, with service activities accounting for about two-thirds of all jobs.

Most migrants from the countryside initially get unskilled manual jobs in the city, in such activities as domestic service, or labouring on building sites. They are often ignorant of their rights as employees and can be exploited by their employers. Many are dismissed from their jobs because they do not measure up to the employer's requirements or because they complain about their pay or working conditions. In the case of construction workers, most are only employed to work on a single building. From the employer's viewpoint there is a considerable advantage in sacking migrants who have grown accustomed to the city, and who have learnt something of their legal rights as employees. In a situation where jobs are scarce and many new migrants are coming to the city in search of work, the employers usually prefer to keep hiring new recruits from the countryside because these people will be less demanding about wages and work conditions. Meanwhile, there is a growing pool of former wage-workers looking for alternative work. Some will return regularly to the countryside to take the jobs available at harvest time. Most, along with thousands of recent school-leavers and newly-arrived migrants hunting for jobs, will have little choice but to work in labour-intensive service occupations in the lower circuit of the economy.

The struggle for jobs and incomes is most evident in the lower circuit of the economy. Many lower circuit service jobs are open to illiterate and unskilled people, and to the very young, the old and the handicapped, all of whom might otherwise find no work at all. Most of these jobs, however, yield only very low incomes, and many of them require long

Fig. 5.11 Garbage pickers at work on the municipal rubbish tip in Cali. In the background squatter houses are being built on river-side land raised above the flood level by the infilling of rubbish.

hours of tedious or exhausting work. The range of lower-circuit service jobs is very large. The commonest are petty trading in the streets, markets or small shops, domestic service, personal services, for example shoe-shining, hair-cutting and radio-repairing, and small-scale transport activities like portering and barrow-pushing. These occupations have a low status and often break local by-laws, but they are generally viewed as respectable. In contrast, a minority of lower circuit service workers engage in activities which are despised or criminal. The despised occupations include begging, prostitution, and scavenging through dustbins and refuse tips (Fig. 5.11). In the criminal category there are many forms of theft, some of them involving violence, and also a variety of offences concerned with trafficking in illegal products.

Many of those whose work is despised or criminal justify the ways in which they make a living by saying that they have no alternative. Others argue that their only alternatives, such as domestic service for girls, or construction labouring for men or women, yield only miserable incomes. Still others point to the wealth of the urban elites and the corruption of some leading officials and businessmen, arguing that society is so unequal and immoral that a poor person has the right to do anything which enables him to make a living. Although a few skilful and lucky criminals may earn relatively high incomes, most criminals and almost all those who engage in despised occupations remain very poor. Those who work scavenging through dustbins or rubbish tips, for example, usually have to put in a long and hard day's work just to get enough money to pay for the cheapest foods needed to feed their families. Their work consists of sifting through the refuse looking for old clothes, bottles, scrap iron, cardboard, newspaper and other products which can be sold to wholesalers for subsequent resale either as second-hand consumer goods or as industrial raw materials. Although they provide a useful service in recovering goods which can be re-used, helping to save scarce raw materials and to hold down living costs for consumers, the work is filthy and dangerous to their health.

The small and irregular earnings of many people working in the lower circuit are such that visiting West Europeans and North Americans often consider the people effectively unemployed or severely underemployed. The work of the poor in South American cities supports an economy and society which operate to concentrate wealth into the hands of a few. Many would argue that such an economy and society relies on the exploitation of the majority of the population, and uses the poor as a reserve of cheap labour which can be employed or dismissed depending on economic circumstances. Such arguments are reinforced by the fact that social security systems are generally available only to those with regular jobs in government departments and large companies, so that they offer no assistance to the poorer members of society. Those who are most likely to suffer hardship and deprivation, therefore, are also those who lack the security of a long-term job contract, sickness and unemployment benefits, free medical care, maternity allowances, an old-age pension and all the other forms of welfare protection which citizens of the First World countries tend to take for granted. Thus, the shortage of reasonable employment and the lack of universal welfare benefits help to explain the poverty of a large part of the urban population and of an even larger proportion of the rural population in South America. In turn, the presence of mass poverty in the cities, alongside the wealth of the richest inhabitants and of the big business companies, helps to explain many of the social problems such as bad housing, petty theft and violent crime.

The struggle for housing and the rise of shanty-towns

The rapid expansion of the city population, the shortage of reasonable employment, and the grinding poverty of many families, lead to a desperate struggle for land and housing. Housing which is cheap enough for the poor is simply not available in sufficient quantities. Because they cannot afford to buy the houses that are available, the poor take to building their own shacks on unguarded areas of empty land. The result is the formation of shanty-towns, which are literally neighbourhoods of shacks, built on the outskirts of most South American cities.

The rapid growth of shanty-towns can be illustrated by the case of Rio de Janeiro in Brazil. Here the shanty-towns are called favelas, and they were first recorded in 1920. Since then, and especially since 1960, the increase in rural–urban migration has led to the rapid growth of favela population. In 1950, the favela population was 8.5 per cent of the city's total population, and by 1960 it was almost 16 per cent. Between 1965 and 1979 Rio de Janeiro's favela population grew from 417,000 to 1,700,000, and therefore increased more than three times in only 14 years. By 1979, instead of being a very small proportion of the city population, the people of the favelas represented 32.2 per cent of those in the city. Now, a third of the people in Rio de Janeiro live in shanty-towns.

The growth of shanty-towns in South America reflects the struggle of millions of individuals to gain a home. When new migrants arrive in the city, they usually stay with friends or relatives in a low-income residential area. Alternatively, they may rent a room in a lodging house near the city centre, where they have the best chances of picking up casual work. Eventually, the squalor of their cramped living conditions, the feeling that they have overstayed their welcome as guests, or the expense of their lodgings, encourages the migrants to move. They will establish their own houses, usually in shanty-towns towards the outskirts of the city. Sometimes a

Fig. 5.12 A peripheral shanty-town in the city of Lima, Peru. The dwellings are relatively widely spaced in the desert. The more established houses are built of mud bricks, while the newer ones further up the hill are built of reed matting. The man pedalling the tricycle rickshaw (right) is an itinerant seller of mattresses.

family will buy an empty patch of land, often where house construction is prohibited by the city planners. Alternatively, they may take part in an invasion, whereby they team up with other people to literally invade an area of land and divide it up for building plots. By working with a group of anything from 5 to 5,000 families, usually at night, each family reduces its chances of being evicted simply because it is surrounded by other invaders. The people become squatters because they have no legal right to the land they occupy. They also become known as shanty-dwellers because their houses are generally shacks built from cheap materials like straw matting and cardboard. Such ways of coping with their own housing problems are not only characteristic of migrants to the city, but also of poor people born in the city itself. They too buy plots and construct illegal buildings, take part in land invasions to establish new shanty-towns, or simply rent or buy property in existing ones.

When hundreds of thousands of people construct their own shanties on empty land, the physical impact on a city is immense. The shanty-towns are made up of shabby clusters and rows of shacks spreading over large areas beyond the more solidly constructed central area of the city. In most cases, the shanty-towns occupy the least desirable land, which is not wanted for farming, factories or good quality housing. After all, as the shanty-dwellers usually occupy the land illegally, they are careful to choose land which seems unused. If shanty-dwellers took over good farming land, the landowners would soon call in the police or even the army to drive them off. Often, therefore, shanty-towns are crowded onto steep hillsides, as in Rio de Janeiro and Caracas, or spread over swamp land or desert. In Guayaquil, Ecuador, the shanties cover large areas of tidal mud flats and former mangrove swamp, where the flimsy wooden huts have to be built on stilts above the water, and where many can only be reached by board walks (see Fig. 5.14). In Lima, the shanty-towns occupy steep rocky hillsides and large tracts of desert. Here, because the invasions have been highly organized and because land is fairly abundant, the shanties are often widely spaced and laid out in a grid plan to leave room for roads (Fig. 5.12). The physical spread and location of shanty-towns, therefore, varies between different South American cities,

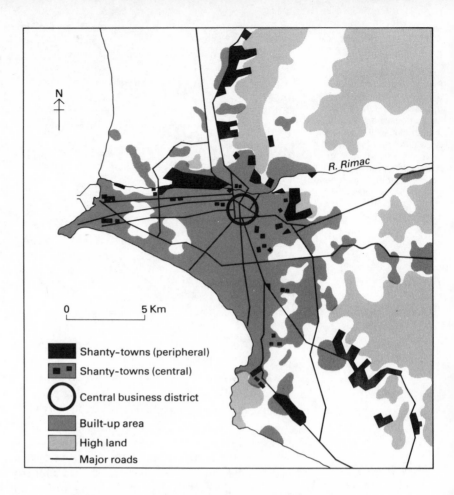

Fig. 5.13 The distribution of shanty-towns in Lima. After Jean-Paul Deler, *Lima 1940–1970: Aspects de la croissance d'une capitale Sud-Amérique,* Centre d'Études de Géographie Tropicale, Bordeaux, 1974.

R. Rimac

0   5 Km

■ Shanty-towns (peripheral)
▪ Shanty-towns (central)
O Central business district
■ Built-up area
■ High land
— Major roads

depending on what empty land is available. The appearance of the shanties themselves also varies, depending largely on what cheap building materials are suitable for the climate. Mud brick and matting walls with flat roofs are typical of Lima's desert shanty-towns, while in Rio de Janeiro the roofs are usually tiled or made of corrugated iron so as to cope with the heavy rainfall.

Some small shanty-towns occupy pockets of land close to a city centre. These are usually the most squalid and miserable, as there is little hope of the city's authorities and property speculators allowing the shacks to remain in a central location. Most shanty-towns, however, occupy large sectors of the outskirts of cities, where their future is more secure. This is illustrated by the case of Lima (Fig. 5.13). In Cali, the poorest, shanty-type houses are on the outer edge of the city, although here local relief has affected the pattern. The wealthy have built the best-quality houses in the more attractive hillside areas on the west of the city (Fig. 5.6). Medium-quality housing occupies the central districts (Fig. 5.7), and the poor are left to build their houses on the low-lying marshy land to the east and in a few areas of steep mountainside to the west (Fig. 5.8).

The illegality, poverty and bad location of most of the shanty-towns mean that public services are either inadequate or simply unavailable, and that health conditions are poor. The most serious problems usually relate to drinking-water supplies and sanitation. In most cities, thousands of babies and small children in shanty-towns die each year from malnutrition, and from infections such as dysentery and pneumonia. The unhealthy conditions are well illustrated by the case of São Paulo, one of the more prosperous cities and certainly the most dynamic of all the large cities on the continent. In São Paulo more than a third of the city's houses, mainly in the peripheral shanty-towns, have no sewer connections or cesspools. Instead the people usually make use of open holes or dry latrines. Most of their drinking water comes from shallow wells, and these are often contaminated by the proximity of the open holes.

The peripheral shanty-towns begin with very poor housing and health conditions, but most of them improve substantially over ten or twenty years. Their inhabitants are generally determined to improve their environment, and many spend much of their spare time and all the money they can save on making improvements to their houses. Thus, over a few years a one-room shack made of old planks, cardboard and corrugated iron might be converted to a two- or three-room brick house with a tile roof. Some residents even add a second or third storey, and many eventually take in lodgers or open a small shop or workshop in the house to make some extra income. Neighbourhood pressure groups are organized to lobby the authorities to legalize the properties and to provide such basic services as roads, drinking water, electricity, sewers, schools, clinics, and bus routes through the area. Considerable effort is put into petitioning the authorities and little by little improvements are achieved. Urban poverty is highly visible and embarrassing to the powerful and wealthy people in the city, particularly when it is criticized by visiting foreigners. The urban poor are also so numerous that demonstrations or riots could eventually threaten the government, and of course their votes are needed when elections are held. Even dictatorships need some signs of popular support in order to maintain their hold on power and impress foreign visitors. For all these reasons, the municipal administrations and national authorities tend to help some of the urban neighbourhood groups by providing a few services and making improvements. In general, the urban poor obtain rather more from their governments than the rural poor. The rural poor are out of sight, and because they are dispersed and isolated, they are less capable of organizing themselves or putting pressure on the authorities.

The waiting period for the installation of public services in the peripheral shanty-towns of South American cities varies considerably from service to service, and between neighbourhoods. Some fortunate areas may be legalized and have most basic services installed within five years of the first shacks being put up, while others may suffer delays of twenty years or more before even one or two public services are provided. Some services, such as main sewer links, may never be installed, and many of the services which are eventually provided prove to be low quality or inadequate. Drinking water for example, may be supplied to standpipes in the street rather than to individual houses, and up to fifty families may have to share a single tap. Most of the services which are provided have to be paid for by the residents, and the shanty-town families undergo considerable hardship both in living without services for many years and then in scraping together the money to pay the bills for the services when they are provided. Nevertheless, there is an air of optimism about many of the peripheral shanty-towns, and they are sometimes described as 'slums of hope' because of the many modest improvements which are made in living conditions (Figs. 5.14–5.16). They contrast very sharply with the smaller shanty-towns and the overcrowded rented tenements closer to the city centre, which are often described as 'slums of despair' because conditions there are very bad and more likely to worsen than to improve.

The pros and cons of urban expansion

All over South America urban expansion is having major economic and social effects, not all of which are beneficial either to the economy or the welfare of the population.

Economic efficiency

The main argument in favour of urban expansion is that of economic efficiency. Cities are seen as the most efficient locations for industry and as the places where public services are provided most efficiently. The economist Lauchlin Currie and the regional planner John Friedmann are known particularly for putting forward this point of view in their writings of the 1960s and early 1970s. They pointed out that as a result of agglomeration economies (see Chapter 4), as well as the concentration of capital investment and skilled workers, the productivity of industry tends to be highest in cities. They also showed that urban expansion can lead to economic efficiency in providing public services. Many public services involve moving something over a distance, whether this is for consumption like drinking water or electricity, or a waste material like sewage. The closer people live together, then the cheaper it usually is to provide them with these services because the length of the networks of roads, pipes, and cables is reduced. Services like public transport, telephones and refuse collection are only moderately expensive to provide for a dense urban population, but extremely expensive to provide for people who live scattered across the countryside. Even when cities become very large, public service provision still remains relatively cheap. In São Paulo, for example, the demand for drinking water is now so great that the authorities need to tap water supplies at a great distance from the city. However, the high density of population in the urban area means that the water is very cheap to distribute, a cost advantage which outweighs the expense of seeking the distant supplies. Other types of public services such as medical and educational facilities are also provided more efficiently for a large urban population than for a rural population. It is only the cities which can maintain the specialist branches of these services, such as intensive care units in hospitals, or university institutes to train industrial engineers. The process of urbanization therefore can facilitate access to services and a better standard of living for the population.

The modernization of society

A second argument in favour of urban expansion is that the move of rural people to the cities has social benefits which in turn assist economic growth. Urban expansion is seen as helping the modernization of society. When people from the countryside move to the cities, they become aware of different attitudes to work, recreation, politics, and family life, and of

Fig. 5.14 The suburbio, the main peripheral shanty-town area, in the city of Guayaquil, Ecuador, where shacks are built on tidal mud flats, in areas of former mangrove swamp. The shacks are approached by board walks until the households can pressurize the authorities to fill in the street line in order to convert the area to dry land. Rubbish and excreta collect in the empty areas between the rows of shacks.

Fig. 5.15 Improvement in progress in the suburbio of Guayaquil. Dump-trucks hired by the municipality are being used to raise the level of the land to form a dirt road. Once the road is complete, other services like piped water and rubbish collection can be introduced, although some-times this takes many years.

Fig. 5.16 This area of the Guayaquil suburbio has passed through the two stages shown in Figs. 5.14 and 5.15. Some of the shanty-dwellers have constructed a second storey. Electricity and a few telephone lines have been installed, but there is still no piped water supply or sewerage system. The shack on the right has just acquired the wooden framework for its second storey.

new opportunities for buying consumer goods. As a result, they change their traditional beliefs, customs and patterns of consumption. In the city, in contrast to the countryside, there is plenty of scope for the exchange of ideas and information, so that improvements are likely to be more rapid. It can also be argued that city life encourages the determination to succeed at work and to improve the standard of living. In these ways, social changes are produced which encourage economic growth by stimulating consumer demand and the provision of goods and services. It is important to realize, however, that the social changes are not necessarily good in all respects. They involve people dropping their distinctive local values and acquiring values characteristic of Western Europe or North America, and these changes may lead to cultural dependency and loss of pride in their identity. Even if the people are materially better off, they may be no happier than they were before. They are now more aware of all the material goods and pleasures that they lack, and they can hardly avoid being envious of the very rich people who live in parts of the city.

The problems associated with urban poverty

The most frequently used argument against urban expansion points to the poverty and bad living conditions of much of the urban population and suggests that improvements can only be achieved in the cities if the inflow of migrants is stopped. It is sometimes even suggested that many of the migrants who have already settled in the cities should be forced to return to their place of origin. The large numbers of workers with very low incomes, the expansion of petty service occupations and the high levels of unemployment (between 5 and 15 per cent of the labour force in most cities) are seen as the result of rapid urban expansion. Other consequences commonly cited are the overcrowding of the inner-city slums, the rapid spread of shanty-towns on the urban periphery, and the bad health and housing of most of the urban poor.

Urban poverty is clearly a serious problem in South American cities, but it does not provide a logical argument against urban expansion. Poverty is not specifically an urban problem, but rather a national and international one. However bad conditions are in the cities, they are generally worse in the towns, and even worse in the countryside. The migrants who come to the cities are not behaving foolishly, but simply moving from where they know conditions are bad to where they believe conditions will be better. In all the South American countries, average rural incomes are lower than average urban incomes, and the urban areas have a greater variety of job opportunities and services. Many rural areas also have serious problems of seasonal unemployment, very bad housing, virtually no public services, and increasing hardship resulting from such factors as soil erosion, recurring drought, and the growing subdivision of smallholdings. Above all, the rural areas suffer from physical isolation. The problem of ill-health for example, may be equally severe in poor rural and poor urban neighbourhoods, but the city people have a major advantage. They can get to a doctor or nurse with relative ease, although they may have great problems scraping together the money to pay for treatment. In contrast, for many rural people even reaching a doctor or nurse may require a long and difficult journey to the nearest major town, and many of the sick and injured die before they can even complete the journey. In such circumstances only the enforcement of rigid government controls to keep people in the rural areas against their will could stop the flow of migrants to the cities. Such controls might eventually reduce the problems of urban poverty, but only at the cost of greatly increasing the more serious problems of rural poverty.

Pollution and congestion

Another argument against urban expansion focuses on what are usually described as the 'diseconomies of agglomeration', factors which work against the agglomeration economies we have already described. The two key diseconomies are pollution and congestion, which increase markedly as cities grow larger. Both pollution and congestion have clear economic costs, the former in terms of increased expenses of cleaning, purification and waste disposal, and the latter in terms of the extra time, transport fares and fuel used because of traffic delays and diversions. In no case, however, is there convincing evidence that these diseconomies outweigh the economic advantages of larger cities. Their main significance is in terms of ill-health, quality of life, and their tendency to increase social inequalities. Most of the pollution, noise and inconvenience falls on the urban poor, as they cannot afford the cost of overcoming such problems. The urban rich can afford to move out to quiet low-density residential areas with good public services, located far from the main industries and traffic routes. In contrast, most of the poor have little choice but to live in overcrowded and dirty conditions, often close to industrial areas and traffic routes, and sometimes by noisy or unpleasant installations like motorway fly-overs, railway shunting yards and sewage farms.

Air pollution is a serious problem resulting from the combination of vehicle exhaust fumes and industrial emissions, particularly in cities enclosed in narrow valleys like Caracas and Medellín, and in cities with dry, sunny climates like Lima and to a lesser extent Santiago. The cities in narrow valleys also tend to have the most serious problems of water pollution and motor vehicle traffic congestion, although congestion is also notable in the three largest cities of the continent, São Paulo, Buenos Aires and Rio de Janeiro. Most of the major city administrations in South America have already spent large sums of money on urban motorways, tunnels and fly-overs so as to reduce traffic congestion (Fig. 5.17). Particularly large investments have been made in Buenos Aires, São Paulo and Santiago in providing underground railway (metro) systems, and similar schemes are well advanced in Rio de Janeiro and Caracas. Such costly urban transport projects impose burdens on local taxpayers, increase reliance on foreign loans, and lead to the demolition or permanent blighting of large housing areas.

Most of those who are concerned about pollution and congestion, and their ill effects on health and the quality of life, suggest that medium-size cities are preferable to very large cities. Those favouring medium-size cities do not agree about the best size, which is usually viewed as somewhere between 250,000 and 1 million population. There is little evidence to justify any particular size, or even to justify their general argument that medium is preferable to very large. However, the view has led to two general policy proposals. First, that cities in the 100,000 to

Fig. 5.17 A complex split-level road junction in Rio de Janeiro. Such reinforced concrete structures require heavy government investment, and are mainly of benefit to the wealthy minority of the population which owns cars.

500,000 range should be encouraged to grow by government investments, and incentives to the private sector. Second, that cities with over a million inhabitants should be strictly controlled by using high taxes, preventing many forms of new investment and withdrawing national government support. These policies have been adopted by several national governments, for example Colombia since 1975, but there is little sign of their being taken seriously. There is bitter opposition from most industrial and political interest groups in the larger cities, and particularly from the multinationals who often threaten to cut off investment altogether if they are not allowed to locate in the largest cities.

The impact on rural areas and peripheral regions

One of the strongest arguments against urban expansion is based on the fact that total resources for investment are limited, and the idea that reducing inequalities is more important for national development than achieving the highest possible levels of economic growth. The heavy concentration of investment in construction, public services, infrastructure, industry, and property in urban areas is seen as depriving the rural and peripheral areas of the country of necessary investments. This leads on to the suggestion that investments should be distributed more evenly throughout the whole country, and that priority should be given to agriculture, rural infrastructure, satisfying the basic needs of the rural population, and building up the nation's human resources through major investment in education and health care for everyone. This proposal is a total reversal of present trends and a strikingly different model of national development. It has been tried out in various countries of the Third World, most notably China, North Korea, Vietnam and Cuba, but it has never been seriously tried in South America. It is a Socialist or Communist model requiring that most production be in the hands of state or communal enterprises, and that the national government has a dominant role in determining the location and types of investment. While multinational and local companies control most of the capital investment in South American countries, and while those countries remain heavily dependent on First World investment and technology, there is no prospect of a major shift in investment to give preference to rural and peripheral areas.

The variety of arguments

The current economic and political system in South America operates on the basis of agglomeration economies, of continuing high levels of economic and social inequality, and on the freedom of internal migration from periphery to core. Only a major political upheaval could change this situation, and this is unlikely during the remainder of the twentieth century. There will be many elections and minor revolutions, but there is unlikely to be a massive transformation in the general style of national development. The groups who benefit from the present system are too powerful to permit more than modest changes, so that the existing policies can be adjusted and made more effective, but not totally transformed. There is no real possibility of preventing migration to the cities, or of reversing investment patterns to produce a major redistribution of wealth to rural and peripheral areas. The arguments for stopping urban expansion, therefore, are unlikely to be supported by effective policies.

Policy discussions on urban growth tend to focus on two sets of issues. First, whether governments should try to slow down urban expansion, should allow it to proceed unrestrained, or should actually try to speed it up. Second, whether governments should attempt to redirect urban expansion away from the large cities towards medium-size cities, or even towards the major towns. Views differ on these policy issues, and the policies adopted so far show considerable variation. In Colombia, for example, the national development plan which ran from 1971 to 1975 set out policies to encourage urbanization and to direct urban expansion mainly to the four largest cities, all with populations of over half a million. In contrast, the 1975–1978 national development plan set out policies to reduce the rate of urbanization through increased investment in selected rural areas, and to channel most urban expansion to 27 'intermediate cities' with populations in the 50,000 to 350,000 range. The 1971–1975 plan was quite effective in achieving its objectives, perhaps because it was simply encouraging existing trends. The 1975–1978 plan, however, had little effect, and the main urban expansion continued to be in the four largest cities.

The problems of planning

Rapid urban expansion has led to many planning problems, which are almost impossible to solve. In any country, planners have difficulty in organizing the growth of a city so that it is satisfactory to the majority of people. Planners in South America, however, do not have the same power as their counterparts in Western Europe or North America. Many different authorities are in charge of different aspects of the city. One office deals with roads, another with sewage, another with electricity, and so on, each in charge of perhaps only a single area of the city. In addition to bureaucratic problems there is a shortage of public money, because property and income taxes do not yield very much, owing to inefficient collection and to the poverty of much of the population. There is just not enough money to provide a whole city with the standard of services expected in Europe or North America. Nevertheless, South American planners tend to aim for the same standards. As a result, they concentrate investments in the city centre and a few rich neighbourhoods, leaving the rest of the city with very inadequate services.

The difficulties which arise because of the large number of authorities involved and because of the lack of public money are made far worse by the rapid growth of the cities. The expanding city populations need housing, drinking water, schools, health facilities and many other services. The squalid character of shanty-towns and other poor housing areas shows that the municipal administrations cannot cope. Much building, particularly of the poorest houses, takes place without planning permission and in areas which the planners want for other land uses. In Bogotá (Colombia) for example, although there has been very little invasion of land, almost half the city's houses have been built without planning permission.

Whenever houses are built illegally, whether or not their owners have a title to the land on which the house is built, the residents usually have no right to public services. In such cases they must do without, or pay private companies to provide services. Drinking water, for example, is supplied by private companies to much of the shanty-town population in Lima and Guayaquil. Sometimes shanty dwellers will take the illegal, and often dangerous, step of tapping the public water supply pipes and electricity cables. An important task for the authorities is to legalize the residents' occupation of the land, usually in return for a payment of money. Depending on who owns the land, and the residents' ability to pay, this legalization may take as long as 20 or 30 years from the time when the land was occupied. Even if the problem of land ownership is ignored, many services are difficult and costly to provide, simply because the houses are built in a disorderly pattern and too close together. It proves impossible to build roads and to install sewers and water pipes without pulling down many of the houses. In addition, the poorest housing is often in areas unsuited to urban expansion, and this makes service provision even more difficult. Drinking-water pipes, for example, are often contaminated if they are laid in marshy areas, and they are very expensive to lay on steep, rocky hillsides (Figs. 5.18 and 5.19).

Some of the problems posed by shanty-town development could be prevented if suitable land were made available for those wanting to build their own houses. Much of the urban and surrounding rural land is held by a wealthy minority, who only sell it when they can make a massive profit. Governments could pass and enforce laws to make landowners sell their land at a lower price. At present, however, no South American governments seem to have the political will to make such changes, and the few urban land reforms that have taken place have had little effect.

Most national governments and municipal administrations have made token attempts to build houses for the urban poor. In general, the projects have helped only a small minority of the urban population, and usually not those in most need. Probably the only realistic way of solving the housing problems of the urban poor, is for the government to confiscate or purchase large areas of land from the owners. That land can then be divided into plots and organized to allow for the easy provision of

Fig. 5.18 A shabby hillside shanty-town in Lima, which lacks piped water, sewers and most other basic services. It is very difficult to provide services on such steep, rocky hillsides and most urban planners would prefer to leave these areas empty.

Fig. 5.19 An improved shanty-town in Lima, which has become one of the lower middle-income housing areas of the city. The area probably looked like Fig. 5.18 fifteen years ago. The costly water-tower on the hill top provides piped water to the neighbour-hood. Initially, however, the water must be pumped up the hill from the main water pipe.

services. Spaces would be left for roads. Sewers, water pipes and electricity cables would be laid before the plots were allocated to individual owners. The new owners would then be allowed and encouraged to build their own houses on the plots. As the owners of the new 'self-help' houses became wealthier, they themselves would improve the quality of their homes and so improve the appearance of the area. However, when governments lack the political will to confiscate and redistribute land, this way of avoiding the problems of shanty-town development needs a lot of public money. The money is generally not being made available, either because governments do not wish to raise the necessary funds by increasing taxation, or because they prefer to spend public money on other projects.

The way in which public money is spent can be viewed as another of the problems of planning in South American cities. The city authorities often choose to fund huge projects which benefit the wealthy few but fail to help the poor majority. For example, instead of using public money to provide sewers for a number of shanty-towns, the authorities may build a six-lane motorway or an expensive new government building. Motorways help the few people rich enough to own cars, and large buildings add to a city's importance, but they do not help the mass of urban poor. The planners in South America are often too ready to copy the road and building projects carried out in North America rather than introduce projects which might be of more use to a city's inhabitants. South American governments have also started ambitious projects to build new cities, partly to reduce overcrowding in the existing cities. The two most important examples are Brasilia, founded in 1960, and Ciudad Guayana established in 1961.

Much of this section so far has focused on what is called physical planning; in other words, planning which deals with things that are built, like houses and roads. Yet the planning problems of South American cities go far beyond those of physical planning. The major problem is to generate employment for the expanding city populations. With good jobs most people could then afford to buy enough food and have decent housing. However, this 'economic' planning has to be carried out in the country as a whole. If the city economy were improved to provide a lot of good jobs, and if housing and services were improved in the poorest urban areas, then many more people would move from the countryside and towns into the city. They would go on moving until the city was again crowded with poor people unable to find satisfactory employment and decent housing. So whatever improvements were made to the city economy and housing, poor people would flood to the city to take advantage of the situation, and their huge numbers would wipe out the effects of the improvements. The city would be as it was before, only much larger. The major problems caused by rapid urban expansion have to be tackled by bringing about change in the country as a whole. While there is still inadequate employment and poverty in the countryside and the towns, there will continue to be inadequate employment and poverty in the major cities.

6 The resource frontiers

The hollow continent

South America is a relatively sparsely populated continent. In 1985, for example, the average population density of South America was only 15 persons per square kilometre, and even Ecuador, the most densely populated country, had fewer than 34 persons per square kilometre. For comparison, Table 6.1 presents information for two of the most densely populated world regions, the European Economic Community (EEC) and South Asia. The average population density of the whole EEC in 1985 was 172 persons per square kilometre, and for the whole of South Asia it was 221. The Netherlands, the most densely populated country in the EEC, had 351 persons per square kilometre, while Bangladesh, the most densely populated country in South Asia, had 701. Compared with these countries, there is certainly no overall shortage of land in South America.

Despite the relative abundance of land in the South American countries, much of the land is not suitable for farming and several countries lack such key natural resources as oil and coal. In comparison with most other continents, however, South America is well-endowed with cultivable land and natural resources. The distinguishing features of South America are the markedly unequal distribution of these amongst the population, and the high proportion of the total resources which is left virtually unused. The continent has so many smallholders and landless rural labourers unable to win access to sufficient land to make a

Table 6.1 Population densities in South America, EEC and South Asian countries, mid-1985

South America Country	Density	EEC Country	Density	South Asia Country	Density
Ecuador	33.1	Netherlands	351	Bangladesh	701
Colombia	24.9	Belgium	318	Sri Lanka	241
Venezuela	19.0	West Germany	246	India	233
Uruguay	17.1	United Kingdom	229	Nepal	118
Chile	16.0	Italy	189	Pakistan	118
Brazil	16.0	Luxembourg	135	Bhutan	27
Peru	14.5	Denmark	119		
Argentina	11.0	France	101		
Paraguay	9.1	Republic of Ireland	51		
Bolivia	5.8				
Guyana	3.8				
Suriname	2.9				
French Guiana	0.8				
All South America	15.0	All EEC	172	All South Asia	221

Countries are listed in rank order of population density.
Population densities are in persons per square kilometre of national territory.

Source: Authors' calculations from *World Bank Atlas 1986* and World Bank, *World Development Report 1987*.

reasonable living, and yet there are also vast areas of potentially cultivable land lying virtually unused.

Over half the continent is uninhabited or has an average population density of under one person per square kilometre. There are many uninhabited and sparsely populated areas in all the South American countries apart from Uruguay, most being zones of barren mountains, desert or swamp with no obvious potential for farming, mining or forestry. Most barren areas lie in the Andes, in desert and swamp zones to the east and west of this mountain chain, and in the cold temperate and sub-polar areas of southern Chile and Argentine Patagonia. In addition to such areas, however, there is an enormous tract of tropical rain forest and adjacent sub-tropical savannas covering most of the basins of the Amazon and Orinoco rivers and much of the Guianas. This vast area is generally uninhabited or sparsely populated, yet unlike such zones as the Atacama Desert or Tierra del Fuego, it is not obviously unsuitable for human settlement, farming, forestry and other economic activities. Together the Amazon and Orinoco basins form a vast near-empty centre to South America, with all the main population concentrations of the continent grouped in an arc around them.

Viewed as a whole, South America seems a 'hollow continent' with many densely populated rural areas, towns and cities around the exterior. This pattern is mainly a reflection of the settlement process and historical development of the continent: conquest and settlement by European colonial powers, and the growth of maritime trading with the First World. For centuries the interior of the continent has seemed remote and inaccessible. Though Spanish and Portuguese explorers penetrated most of the Amazon and Orinoco basins during the sixteenth and seventeenth centuries, these tropical areas were unattractive to European settlers. They did not have the mineral wealth or available labour force of the Andes, nor the suitability for European-type agriculture of such areas as the central valley of Chile or the Argentine Pampas. In addition, their hot, humid climates were unpleasant and unhealthy for Europeans, and the native Indians were viewed as primitive and warlike. Some European settlements were established in the interior of the continent during the colonial period, but almost all remained small or were eventually abandoned.

Geopolitics and national security

Although land in South America is abundant relative to population, there have been many struggles between countries to gain the richest and best located resources, and also to enlarge their territories. Since the early nineteenth century the independent countries of South America have engaged in numerous minor conflicts and several serious wars, most notably the War of the Triple Alliance (Paraguay against Argentina, Uruguay and Brazil, 1865–1870), the War of the Pacific (Chile against Peru and Bolivia, 1879–1883), the Chaco Wars (Paraguay against Bolivia, 1929–1935), and the Ecuadorian–Peruvian War of 1941.

Each territorial dispute in South America has concerned the rights of countries to control adjacent more sparsely-populated or uninhabited areas. The Chaco Wars, for example, concerned Paraguayan–Bolivian rivalry for control over the sparsely-populated, but potentially oil-rich,

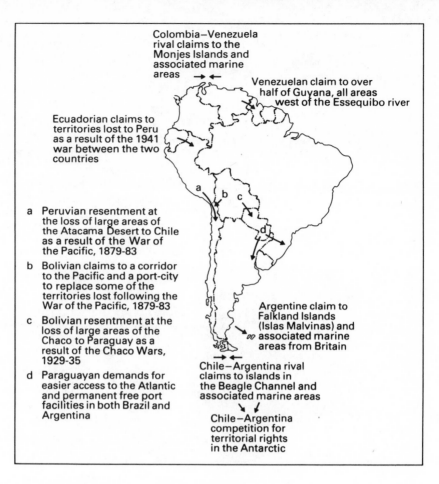

Fig. 6.1 The main territorial disputes and claims in South America.

Colombia–Venezuela rival claims to the Monjes Islands and associated marine areas

Venezuelan claim to over half of Guyana, all areas west of the Essequibo river

Ecuadorian claims to territories lost to Peru as a result of the 1941 war between the two countries

a   Peruvian resentment at the loss of large areas of the Atacama Desert to Chile as a result of the War of the Pacific, 1879-83

b   Bolivian claims to a corridor to the Pacific and a port-city to replace some of the territories lost following the War of the Pacific, 1879-83

c   Bolivian resentment at the loss of large areas of the Chaco to Paraguay as a result of the Chaco Wars, 1929-35

d   Paraguayan demands for easier access to the Atlantic and permanent free port facilities in both Brazil and Argentina

Argentine claim to Falkland Islands (Islas Malvinas) and associated marine areas from Britain

Chile–Argentina rival claims to islands in the Beagle Channel and associated marine areas

Chile–Argentina competition for territorial rights in the Antarctic

Gran Chaco region between the two countries. Similarly, the War of the Pacific concerned rivalry between Chile and Peru and Bolivia for control over the sparsely-populated, but nitrate-rich Atacama desert. The fact that a particular area of the continent has never attracted much settlement has not prevented it from being the focus of territorial disputes. A country can gain many advantages from having a larger territory. The further the frontiers can be extended from the more densely populated areas of the country, the longer it would take an enemy to penetrate these areas and to overcome the armed forces. Moreover, the larger the national territory, the more natural resources are available.

The blend of geography and politics which concerns the rights of countries to particular territories and the achievement of military control over such territories is generally known as geopolitics. Geopolitics play a major part in the foreign and regional development policies of many South American governments. Fig. 6.1 shows at least ten major territorial disputes and claims active in the late 1980s, any of which might flare into war. In addition, more and more South American countries are following the lead taken by Chile, Peru and Ecuador in 1952 by proclaiming a 200-mile maritime territorial limit. Such extensions of territory are intended to establish national rights over fishing and the resources of the seabed. Intruding foreign fishing boats are often arrested, provoking conflicts between countries. More serious sources of conflict, however, are the disputes between Argentina and Chile over the

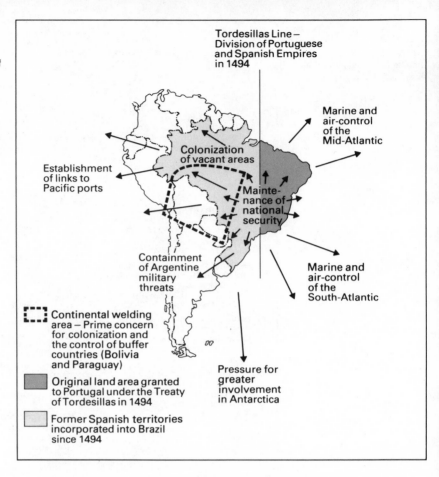

Fig. 6.2 A summary of the principal geopolitical aims of selected Brazilian military leaders.

Tordesillas Line – Division of Portuguese and Spanish Empires in 1494

Marine and air-control of the Mid-Atlantic

Colonization of vacant areas

Establishment of links to Pacific ports

Mainte-nance of national security

Containment of Argentine military threats

Marine and air-control of the South-Atlantic

Continental welding area – Prime concern for colonization and the control of buffer countries (Bolivia and Paraguay)

Original land area granted to Portugal under the Treaty of Tordesillas in 1494

Former Spanish territories incorporated into Brazil since 1494

Pressure for greater involvement in Antarctica

orientation of their frontier in the Beagle Channel south of Tierra del Fuego, the Argentine claim to the British-controlled Falkland Islands, which led to a brief war in 1982, and Chilean–Argentine rivalry in Antarctica. Each of these issues involves the rights to the potential rich marine resources of large tracts of the South Atlantic and the Antarctic Ocean.

No discussion of geopolitics in South America would be complete without a mention of Brazil: the South American country which has been most successful in extending its territory. The main elements of Brazilian geopolitics are summarized in Fig. 6.2. Since the original Tordesillas demarcation of the limits of the Spanish and Portuguese colonial empires in 1494, the territory of Brazil has more than doubled. Brazil now controls almost four-fifths of the Amazon basin. The remaining five Amazon basin countries: Bolivia, Peru, Ecuador, Colombia and Venezuela, have all lost large areas to Brazil since their independence. Since 1964, the Brazilian government has shown special concern for national security, combining expansionist foreign policies with the suppression of internal opposition. The government has deliberately promoted settlement and road-building in frontier areas. Power has been centralized on the national government, thus weakening regional and municipal administrations. Similar policies have been followed since the early or mid 1970s by right-wing regimes in other South American countries, most notably Chile, Argentina, Uruguay, Paraguay and Bolivia.

Territorial integration and the persistence of regional inequalities

In every South American country, particularly Brazil, government concern for geopolitics and national security has led to attempts to 'integrate' the national territory. Integration, in this context, refers to policies to link together the different regions of the country, to ensure that all regions are populated mainly by loyal citizens, and to occupy frontier areas so as to prevent the penetration of settlers or military forces from neighbouring countries. Concern for integration has led to the huge highway projects in the Amazon basin, and also to the settlement of such areas as the Brazilian Mato Grosso and the Colombian and Venezuelan Llanos. The establishment of Brasília as the new capital of Brazil in 1960, shifting the centre of government from Rio de Janeiro in the South-East to the Centre-West region was a project for national integration. It was a first major step towards a more comprehensive occupation of the Amazon basin.

Although territorial integration has been a major objective of South American governments since the 1930s, many factors have prevented its full success. One factor, perhaps the most important, is the high cost of infrastructure in remote and sparsely-populated regions, particularly the high cost of building and maintaining thousands of kilometres of roads. This problem is especially great because these regions yield very little tax revenue to help towards the costs, and because there are too few inhabitants to have a major political influence. Simply to stay in power governments generally have to make most of their investments in the more densely-populated regions, where most citizens live. Such regions benefit from the forces of circular and cumulative causation, and in many cases their comparative advantage over remote and sparsely-populated regions has continued to increase. Indeed, even the little wealth which is yielded by the peripheral regions is mainly reinvested in core areas, and the national periphery is characterized by an unstable and exploitative economy rather than by the conditions necessary for continuing economic growth.

Most population migration in South America is towards the major cities and core regions, rather than towards the uninhabited and sparsely-populated regions of the continent. This migration has accompanied a major shift in economic activity from primary production towards manufacturing, construction, and services. Policies intended to open up new areas of the South American countries are therefore going against national trends, particularly as the new areas are likely to be used mainly for primary production. In many cases, the opening up of new areas for primary production also runs contrary to simple economic principles of comparative advantage, as producers in the new areas cannot compete with the established producing regions. Transport costs from the remote, peripheral regions are too high to justify production for major national or international markets, and producers are also hampered by the lack of local infrastructure.

As a result of the difficulties in encouraging settlement in peripheral regions, and the attractions of core regions, many South American countries have achieved little more, in terms of national integration, than a small expansion of settlement in areas next to existing settled areas, and the establishment of various frontier outposts, most of them simply air-supplied military camps. Between the settled areas and the frontier outposts remain large areas of uninhabited or sparsely-populated forest, savanna, desert or mountains. Such areas sometimes experience a sudden influx of temporary settlers if a major natural resource is discovered, but there is little sign yet that they are likely to undergo large-scale, permanent settlement. Indeed, many of the sparsely-populated areas of the continent are currently losing population because of migration to towns within the peripheral regions and to the major cities in the national core regions. Even in Brazilian Amazonia, where the most spectacular progress was made in opening up new lands for settlement in the 1970s, the most striking population growth has been in a few cities, particularly Belém, Manaus and Cuiabá. Many of the farming areas which were newly settled in the early 1970s are already losing population, and progress in the settlement of further areas is limited, falling far short of government plans.

The search for oil, minerals and other natural resources

Most of the uninhabited and sparsely-populated areas of South America present some possibilities for the discovery and exploitation of oil, minerals, and other valuable natural resources. The search for these resources has been a significant factor in provoking territorial disputes over such areas, and in encouraging road-building and colonization.

The most sought-after new resource in South America is oil. National surpluses and deficits of oil have had a major impact on many other aspects of resource use, and on the settlement of peripheral regions. Of all the South American countries, only Venezuela has oil reserves well in excess of national needs. There, the relative prosperity resulting from the oil export economy has encouraged urbanization. It has also acted as a major disincentive, both to agricultural colonization in peripheral regions and to the search for alternative energy sources. Venezuela has massive reserves of heavy crude oil in the Orinoco oil belt and the Maracaibo Basin which can be brought into commercial production. Even when these reserves are exhausted, Venezuela has substantial areas of oil shales and tar sands which might be used as a source of oil, given relatively high energy prices and the development of new technologies for extraction. Venezuela is therefore likely to remain a major oil exporter well into the twenty-first century.

In sharp contrast to Venezuela's optimistic situation is Brazil, the country with by far the largest oil deficit in South America. Of all the South American countries, Brazil's economy has been most seriously affected by the major price rises in oil which have occurred since 1972. The model of economic development established in Brazil after the change of government in 1964 was heavily based on the expansion of motor vehicle production for the internal market, and on the promotion of road transport. Oil consumption rose considerably and by the mid 1970s it was obvious that major policy changes would be required to avoid the rapid increase of balance of payments deficits and the end of economic growth. Policy changes have been made in three main directions: in attempting to find new oil reserves, in developing new energy sources, and in opening up new mineral and forest reserves with a view to boosting national exports and reducing some imports. These

Fig. 6.3 Drilling for oil in a forest clearing in north-eastern Ecuador. The drilling is being done by specialist foreign firms contracted by Texaco Petroleum, one of the world's largest multinational companies.

efforts have had a major impact on the peripheral regions of the country and on the opening up of Amazonia. The search for new oil reserves has been intensified, both offshore in the Atlantic Ocean and in the Amazon basin, though so far with only modest success. The development of new energy sources has concentrated on three main fields: the nuclear programme discussed in Chapter 1 (see Fig. 1.1), the construction of major hydroelectric projects, most notably Itaipu on the Paraguayan border (see Fig. 4.7), and the promotion of alcohol production from sugar-cane and manioc as a substitute for petrol in powering motor vehicles. The opening up of new mineral and forest reserves has been closely linked with increased road-building and land sales in Amazonia during the 1970s. This has helped the expansion of agribusinesses such as Jari (see Fig. 3.8), the granting of large timber concessions to Brazilian and foreign firms, and the start of large-scale mining schemes such as the Carajás iron ore project about 500 km south-west of Belém, and the

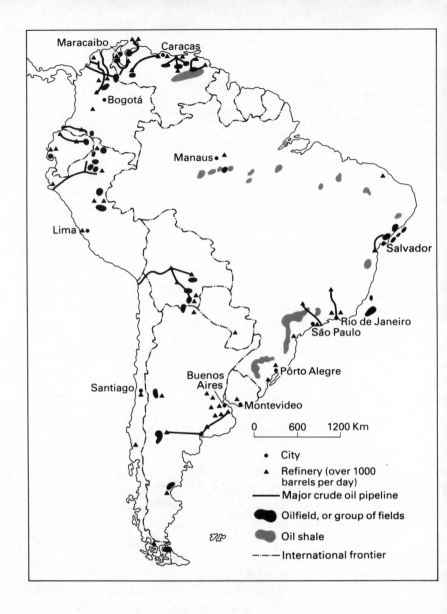

Fig. 6.4 Principal oilfields, pipelines, and refineries in South America, 1980. After *International Petroleum Encyclopedia 1980*.

Legend:
- • City
- ▲ Refinery (over 1000 barrels per day)
- — Major crude oil pipeline
- Oilfield, or group of fields
- Oil shale
- —·—·— International frontier

Scale: 0   600   1200 Km

Trombetas bauxite and aluminium refining project about 900 km west of Belém.

Oil exploration is widespread in South America (Figs. 6.3 and 6.4), in both relatively densely-populated areas and also in uninhabited and sparsely-populated areas. Overall, however, the trend is toward exploration in more remote areas, particularly along the eastern fringe of the Andes, in the extreme south of the continent, and offshore from Brazil's Atlantic coast. With the exception of Venezuela, which has consistently had a large oil surplus, and Chile, which has consistently had an oil deficit, the countries along the Andes (Colombia, Ecuador, Peru, Bolivia and Argentina) have oscillated between oil-surplus and oil-deficit since the early 1950s. Bolivia and Colombia also have large reserves of natural gas for future export. In contrast, Chile and the countries away from the Andes (Brazil, Paraguay, Uruguay and the Guianas) have generally been unable to satisfy their own requrements and seem unlikely to achieve self-sufficiency during the late twentieth century.

Overall, South America is heavily reliant on oil as a source of fuel, and alternatives such as coal and hydroelectric power fall far short of oil in usage. Recent world price rises in crude oil and petroleum products have had an effect not only on Venezuela's oil exploitation prospects and on Brazilian economic growth, but on the economies and patterns of regional development in all the South American countries. New interest is being shown in resource surveys of peripheral regions, and in expanding production from alternative energy sources such as the coal reserves of northern Colombia and those of southern Chile and Argentina. There has also been a major reassessment of the continent's rivers as an energy source. As a result, large-scale hydroelectric schemes are in construction or under study at increasingly great distances from the main electricity consuming areas, for example at Yacyretá on the Argentine–Paraguayan border, and at Tucuruí on the Tocantins River, 250 km south-west of Belém in Brazil. Finally, there is a growing interest in the energy potential of the continent's tropical forests, particularly in Amazonia. Experimental projects are at an early stage, but there are already proposals for the large-scale deforestation of Amazonia to make way for the commercial production of fast-growing plants to produce cellulose, fuel alcohol (from manioc), or vegetable oils for use as diesel oil substitutes (e.g. from the Brazilian dendê palm).

Pioneer colonization

So far, we have concentrated on the military, governmental and major resource exploitation factors affecting the occupation of remote, uninhabited or sparsely-populated regions of South America. Such factors explain the presence of military camps, military and government transport infrastructure, and major mines, agribusinesses, oil installations and other large capital investments belonging to government and multinational corporations. Particularly in the humid tropical areas of the continent, however, the most important single factor in the occupation of new lands is pioneer colonization. This is the settlement of large numbers of relatively small-scale farming and trading families on areas of land which were previously unused or which had only been used for very extensive and low-productivity economic activities.

Pioneer colonization can be of three main types: 'spontaneous', 'semi-directed', and 'directed'. Spontaneous colonization has no significant government involvement in the early stages. Settlers move into an area and establish farms without government support, though after a few years there is usually government involvement in the granting of land titles and in providing such basic services as schools and roads. Semi-directed colonization represents an effort by the government to promote and assist settlement without taking on the full cost and responsibility. The government, for example, might build roads into potential colonization areas and offer land titles and technical assistance to colonists, leaving the colonist families to build their own houses, clear their own land, and find the money to buy tools, seeds and other necessary materials. By contrast, in directed colonization schemes, virtually everything is provided at the outset by the government, so that colonists are recruited, equipped with houses, tools, etc., and instructed on how to establish their own farms. Although directed colonization schemes have been tried in almost all the

South American countries, they are too costly and difficult to apply on a large scale. In general, therefore, colonization is either spontaneous or semi-directed, with the government's initial role usually being the construction of roads in potential or actual colonization areas.

Trends on the continental scale

It is important to recognize that the continent was populated long before the arrival of the Spanish and Portuguese, and that colonization has often been as much the displacement of indigenous peoples by outside intruders as the settlement of truly empty lands. In general, the later-settled areas did not have dense concentrations of indigenous peoples, even in the sixteenth century. Since the Spanish and Portuguese conquests, the sparse population of these areas has diminished because of disease and armed conflicts with outsiders. Such problems have increased with the arrival of new farmer—settlers, and in most cases the pioneer settlement process has accelerated the decline of the indigenous population.

In the nineteenth and early twentieth centuries, most colonization in South America was taking place in the Argentine and Uruguayan Pampas, the Brazilian South, along the Amazon river, and on the outer fringes of the Andes. Subsequently, however, colonization has penetrated most of the Centre-West of Brazil (the Mato Grosso savannas), and large parts of the Amazon and Orinoco basins. Most of the recent colonization in these two basins has been associated with road-building, and roadside settlements have largely replaced riverside settlements as the main centres of economic activity.

In general, the temperate-climate colonization areas of South America, such as the Pampas and the Brazilian South, have been settled permanently and have acquired a prosperous economy based on farming. In contrast, most of the tropical colonization areas have suffered from 'boom and bust' colonization activity, with rapid expansions of settlement during favourable periods and sharp economic and population declines during unfavourable periods. The rubber boom was an extreme case of this phenomenon. From the mid-nineteenth century until the First World War, many settlers came to Amazonia to tap wild rubber in the forests. Many new settlements and riverboat routes were established, tying many of the remoter areas in the Amazon basin into world trade networks. Eventually, however, rubber seeds were taken from the Amazon basin to South-East Asia, where massive plantations were established, undercutting the price of Amazonian wild rubber and effectively ending the boom by 1920.

The pattern of 'boom and bust' in the Amazon and Orinoco basins relates not only to rubber, but also to other natural forest products, and to various minerals, particularly gold. In most cases, however, little has remained from the boom period to stimulate any effective long-term regional development. The fortunes made have generally been reinvested in the core regions of South American countries, or in Europe or North America. It is usually argued that plantation production cannot succeed in the Amazon or Orinoco basins because of the lack of a large, willing and cheap labour force similar to that available in most Asian countries. Indeed, some specialists even suggest that Amazonia's historical tradition of 'boom and bust' is so long- and well-established that the prospects of permanent, productive settlement are very poor. They point to the historical tradition of a 'hollow' and 'moving' frontier of resource exploitation in Amazonia, and to the present drift of population towards the metropolitan areas of South America, and then suggest that successful, lasting pioneer colonization in Amazonia is highly unlikely.

The Brazilian expansion into Amazonia

The most significant wave of pioneer colonization in South America since the Second World War has been the Brazilian 'assault on the Amazon' in the 1970s. The government policies involved were largely worked out in the 1960s, reflecting pressures for geopolitical expansion, national security, territorial integration and the exploitation of new natural resources. Major investments were announced in 1970 after a visit by the President of Brazil to the drought zones of the North-East. The main investment was the Transamazon Highway, a 5,400 km road link from João Pessoa and Recife in the North-East through to the Peruvian frontier. From Recife as far as the 2,600 km Belém–Brasilia Highway, which had been completed in 1960, the Transamazon Highway was nothing more than a renaming and modest improvement of existing roads. From the Belém–Brasilia Highway westward, however, it was to be a completely new road opening up a vast area of tropical rain forest 100 to 500 km south of the Amazon river. Most of the Transamazon Highway was completed by the late 1970s, as a two-lane dirt road linking up to the southern Perimetral Highway, which had been built between the early 1950s and late 1970s to link Brasilia and Cuiabá, in the Mato Grosso, to Rio Branco and beyond.

The broad strategy behind the construction of the Transamazon Highway was to provide a route for the migration of poor northeastern farmers and landless labourers to colonize parts of the Amazon basin, so relieving population pressure in the north-east. It was also planned as an alternative to the existing penetration routes of Amazonia: the Amazon river, the Belém–Brasilia Highway, and the Southern Perimetral Highway, which had been completed from Brasilia as far as Porto Velho by 1965. Directed (planned) colonization schemes were begun between Marabá and Itaituba on the Transamazon Highway, and also around Rondônia on the Southern Perimetral Highway (Fig. 6.5). There was further road-building to provide feeder roads in directed colonization areas and also to complete two major north–south roads, the 1,670 km Cuiabá–Santarém Highway, and the Porto Velho–Manaus–Boa Vista Highway, the latter linking through to Venezuela. Despite the difficult terrain for road-building, and the remoteness of Amazonia from the core regions of Brazil, road-construction proceeded rapidly in the 1970s, with all of the major highways so far mentioned being more or less completed by the end of the decade. One further big project, however, the 4,215 km Northern Perimetral Highway, was only started in a few areas, and this road is unlikely to be completed much before the year 2000.

The Transamazon Highway and the other major roads constructed in Brazilian Amazonia in the 1970s were built with heavy machinery (Fig. 6.6) but, to save cost, were left without bridges over the major rivers (Figs. 6.7 and 6.8). The roads have reasonable driving surfaces, but there can be long delays for vehicles, both at river crossings and whenever a

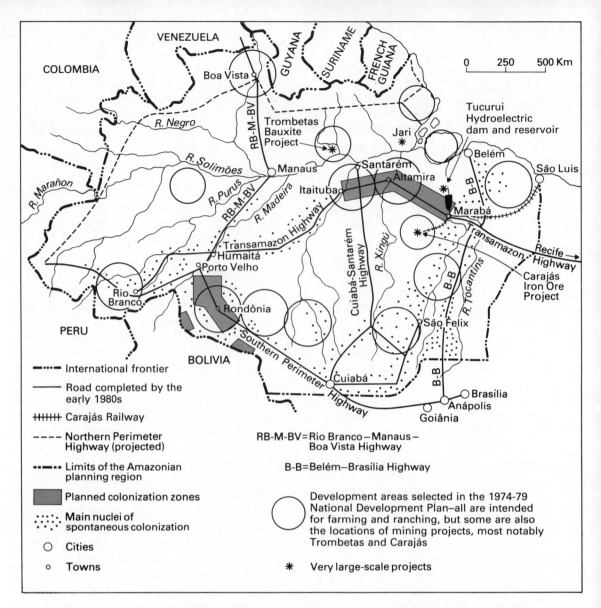

Fig. 6.5 Roads, colonization and major investment projects in Brazilian Amazonia.

flash flood or landslide blocks the way. The directed colonization settlements have not proved very successful, and many of the original government-selected colonists have abandoned their farms and moved into the Amazonian towns, back to the North-East or to the national core regions. In contrast, there has been considerable demand by multinational companies and Brazilian investors to buy up large tracts of land for speculative purposes or to establish agribusinesses, and there has also been a notable influx of spontaneous colonists, particularly from the South-East region to the zone around Rondônia. The overall result is that, even in an area as large as Brazilian Amazonia, there are major land conflicts between the spontaneous colonists, planned colonists, land speculators, agribusinesses, and surviving indigenous tribal groups.

The 1974–1979 Brazilian National Development Plan included grandiose schemes for the settlement and economic development of fifteen selected areas in Amazonia (Fig. 6.5), but many projects were delayed or cancelled and the rate of road-building and new settlement has declined further since then. Many of the areas settled in the early 1970s are proving to be of fairly low soil fertility and isolated

Fig. 6.6 Large bulldozers being used to clear away trees and move earth for road-building in Brazilian Amazonia. Such sophisticated machinery is very effective for rapid road construction, but it is expensive, often imported, provides relatively little employment, destroys valuable timber, and encourages rapid soil erosion.

from suitable markets for agricultural produce. Given the enormous distances, averaging over 3,000 km, from the newly-settled areas to the main national markets for farm produce, few crops can be produced economically for anything more than a local market. Indeed, most farmers have concentrated heavily on cattle and subsistence crops. The few cash crops which have proved relatively successful have been low-bulk, high-value products, such as black pepper. The main emphasis of Amazonian economic expansion has shifted away from agricultural colonization towards cattle ranching, large-scale commercial lumbering, and above all mining and energy projects such as Trombetas, Carajás and Tucuruí.

East from the Andes

The areas of the Andean countries in the humid tropical Amazon and Orinoco basins have sometimes been described as 'East of the Andes and

Fig. 6.7 The ferry where the Transamazon Highway crosses the river Xingú in Brazilian Amazonia. On average the highway crosses one such major river every 200 kilometres.

Fig. 6.8 Part of the queue of vehicles stretching back about half a kilometre waiting to use the river Xingú ferry. Drivers have to wait anything from an hour to several days to make each crossing. The ferries are too small and problems are sometimes accentuated when the ferry's motors break down, or when there is a flood and the ferry cannot operate.

west of nowhere', a saying which reflects their grave isolation from national and international markets. In Venezuela, Colombia, Ecuador and Peru, most agricultural expansion since the Second World War has been north and west of the Andes in the various coastal lowlands, rather than eastward into the Orinoco and Amazon basins. The coastal areas are generally more fertile and much more accessible to markets than the interior lowlands. In Ecuador and Peru, the agricultural expansion of the coastlands has been a major factor in national economic growth, with the large-scale production and export of such crops as bananas, cocoa, coffee, rice, cotton and sugar.

Only Bolivia has had a major wave of eastward colonization, reflecting the fact that the country has had no coastal territories since the War of the Pacific. For Bolivia eastward expansion is the only means of increasing tropical agricultural output. Most of the expansion has been around the city of Santa Cruz, which has become the most prosperous area, with the most rapid rates of population growth in the whole country. The Santa Cruz area has more fertile soils than most other areas east of the Andes in South America. It also has substantial reserves of oil and gas. The Bolivian government's regional development and investment

Fig. 6.9 One of the principal road links between Andean Peru and the eastern lowlands. The road has been built along the narrow canyon of one of the Amazon tributaries. The valley is so narrow that the road has had to be cut in solid rock, with a large overhang above. In such areas road-building is expensive and the roads are frequently blocked by landslides, river erosion and flooding.

policies since the 1950s have emphasised the creation of a growth axis running from La Paz and Oruro on the Altiplano, through Cochabamba and Santa Cruz to Corumbá on the Brazilian frontier. The Santa Cruz area has benefited the most from this road–rail axis, with a major influx of highland migrants and the large-scale expansion of agriculture producing a wide range of cash crops and livestock. The main crops are rice, cotton, sugar and coca. The coca is used both for legal consumption by the Altiplano Indians, and for illegal cocaine trafficking to North America and Western Europe.

The colonization of the Andean fringe areas stretching from northern Bolivia to central Venezuela has been slow in comparison with Brazilian Amazonia, and it has been fragmented between many different penetration roads. Most of these roads are poor quality with frequent problems of landslides and mudflows, yet their construction costs have been high because of the difficult terrain to be crossed (Fig. 6.9). Wherever roads have been constructed, spontaneous colonists have generally moved in to establish small farms. In contrast, most of the roadless areas east of the Andes remain without settlement, or are inhabited only by indigenous tribal groups, a few missionary communities and, close to the frontiers, by air-supplied military garrisons.

Social and economic conditions in humid tropical colonization areas

Even including such long-settled tropical colonization areas as the Guayas basin in coastal Ecuador and the Magdalena Valley in Colombia, the total population of all humid tropical colonization areas in South America was less than 20 million in 1980. Given that the actual and potential tropical colonization areas cover over half the total land area of the continent, average population densities are very low and large zones are entirely uninhabited (Fig. 6.10). In general, the most important problems faced by agricultural colonists are the rigours and hazards of the local environment. In addition they have to cope with the physical and social isolation, distance from markets and sources of supplies, and the lack or inadequacy of public services.

Fig. 6.10 An aerial view of the river Aguarico and nearby forests in the Amazonian lowlands of eastern Ecuador. Despite the widespread deforestation since 1960, most of the Amazon basin still looks like this. Broad rivers with numerous islands and sandbanks flow through huge tracts of largely uninhabited rain forest.

Fig. 6.11 Yanomani women preparing bitter manioc for a festival at a communal house in the Catrimani Valley in northern Brazil. The Yanomani are the largest group of Amazonian Indians who still live in their traditional area.

The hazards facing the newly-arrived agricultural colonists range from such relatively rare events as attacks by native Indians (Fig. 6.11) to the more frequent problems of tropical diseases, unhygienic living conditions without drinking water or sanitation, accidents with axes and saws, and bites from poisonous snakes. For the spontaneous colonist and for many semi-directed colonists, there are also major problems in staking and defending a claim to land, and subsequently in obtaining a legal title to that land from government agencies. Land disputes between colonists are frequent, and small-scale colonists are sometimes displaced from the land that they have laboriously cleared by large-scale estate owners and land speculators.

In the early stages of agricultural colonization, intense effort is required to build a house and to clear enough land to plant a first crop, usually of

Fig. 6.12 A newly-established roadside farm in north-eastern Ecuador, cleared eight months before this photograph was taken, and planted with maize and manioc. The house has a timber frame, split bamboo cane walls and a thatched roof. The farmers (two brothers) claim ownership of 50 hectares of forest. They hope to clear this forest by hand, using axes and machetes, at a rate of two hectares per year.

Fig. 6.13 The main street in the town of Quinindé, one of the principal colonization centres in the northern coastal lowlands of Ecuador. The town is growing rapidly and has much commercial activity.

plantains, maize and manioc (Fig. 6.12). The crucial problem is to ensure that enough subsistence foods are grown on the newly-cleared land before the colonist runs out of supplies and of money to buy food. In most cases, the colonist has to put up with a monotonous and nutritionally-inadequate diet for several years before production can be expanded and diversified to include a greater variety of subsistence and cash crops. Further problems result from the small size of most colonization settlements, their lack of services and recreational activities, and from the considerable distances which must be travelled to reach a town (Fig. 6.13).

In the vast Amazon and Orinoco basins, where the total population was less than 10 million in 1980, the problems faced by agricultural colonists are particularly acute. The problems, however, are even greater for the native Indian groups, and some tribes are now extinct. Some groups lead a miserable existence near the new settlements, scraping a living as servants, labourers, beggars or prostitutes. Some have accepted a docile life as mission converts. Other groups have retreated further into the forests, moving towards inferior hunting and gathering environments under the pressures of the advancing colonists, road-builders, lumbermen, prospectors and soldiers. Violent conflicts between the Indians and these various intruders have been common, as some Indians have taken to arms in a last desperate attempt to preserve their own lands and cultures.

Environmental consequences of humid tropical colonization

The humid tropics of South America include a wide variety of different environments. Most settlement in the region has failed to relate to this diversity, and there has been little care in the selection of areas for colonization and of appropriate forms of land use for those areas. Instead, colonization has tended to be indiscriminate, failing to utilize effectively the potentials of the local environment, and settling unsuitable areas.

In general, where roads have been built in uninhabited and sparsely-populated areas, settlement has preceded, accompanied or followed the road-building. In most cases, however, the selection of road routes has paid little or no attention to the potential of areas near the routes for possible settlement. The result has been the clearing of many steep hillsides and barren soils which should have been left under forest cover to prevent rapid soil erosion. Even where slopes and soils are suitable for farming, inappropriate varieties of plants and animals are often used instead of adequately acclimatized strains. A further problem in many areas has been the continuous cultivation of a single crop, depleting soil fertility in a few years, when a rotation or combination of crops might have retained or even increased fertility.

In most humid tropical colonization areas in South America serious problems have resulted from deforestation, an over-emphasis on cattle farming for beef production, and the failure to plant sufficient tree crops. Most notable are the rapid increases in run-off, leaching, sheetwash and gullying, leading to the reduction of agricultural potential, widespread soil erosion, flash floods and even a decrease in average rainfall because of the reduction in evapotranspiration. One well-known book on these environmental probems was entitled *Amazon jungle: green hell to red desert?*, so as to dramatize the extent of changes taking place. The idea of converting such a vast area to desert is far-fetched, but there is certainly a shift towards more seasonal rainfall patterns and towards savanna and scrub forest. Some experts even speculate that, if rapid forest clearance continues, there will be a major reduction in the world's range of plant and animal species, a drop in the oxygen content of the world's atmosphere, and a shift of the global wind systems producing significant climatic changes in other parts of the world. Whether such dramatic changes could or will take place is highly debatable, but there is undoubtedly a danger that the productive potential and fertility of vast areas will be heavily reduced by inappropriate forms of land use. Such long-term losses greatly outweigh the short-term gains of inappropriate and exploitative forestry and farming. The pattern of 'boom and bust' resource exploitation still continues in the humid tropical colonization areas of South America, and there are grave dangers that contemporary greed will sharply reduce the resources available to future generations.

7 What development ?. . . and for whom?

It is no easy task to assess the development of South America. The continent has undergone a very wide variety of changes over a long and complex history, and there are sharp differences between the experiences of the various countries and regions. Particular changes are interpreted in different ways by different people and there is no single, widely-accepted method for producing a comprehensive assessment. Any assessment, therefore, is a matter of personal opinion, with value judgments made on available information. In general, those who benefit from present conditions and recent changes tend to praise the situation and to suggest that real improvement is occurring. In contrast, those who suffer because of the present conditions and recent changes tend to condemn the situation and to suggest that circumstances are deteriorating. Thus better-off groups tend to have a very positive view and worse-off groups a negative view. Of course, those who hold power tend to justify their own efforts, saying how good the situation is. Those in political opposition tend to criticise and complain, saying how bad the situation is and how much better it could be with different leadership.

The long-term historical view

Making a broad assessment, we suggest that on balance, development in South America was overwhelmingly negative in the sixteenth and seventeenth centuries, but since then it has generally been slightly favourable.

The negative balance of development in the sixteenth and seventeenth centuries reflects the tremendous human suffering and environmental damage which resulted from the conquest. The Spanish and Portuguese inflicted crushing military defeats on the indigenous Indian population. They brought diseases, took land from the Indians, forced massive migrations of population, and extracted large amounts of goods and labour as tax payments. They encouraged the cruel trade in Negro slaves from Africa. Many mineral resources were rapidly exhausted, and in some areas there was a fall in soil fertility and forest cover as a result of exploitative farming and deforestation. Parts of the continent have never regained the levels of agricultural productivity which existed before the conquest. Many of the fine settlements, networks of bridle-paths, irrigation canals and terraces constructed by the Indian civilizations fell into decay (Fig. 7.1).

Even in the sixteenth and seventeenth centuries, however, not all the changes which occurred were negative. The Spanish and Portuguese introduced a variety of important new crops and livestock, the arts of writing and printing, and numerous new technologies, in particular the use of the wheel. They directed the construction of large colonial towns. They also brought Christianity, together with their own skills and values based on European civilization. From a European viewpoint at least,

119

Fig. 7.1 The Peruvian shore of Lake Titicaca. The terraces date from the pre-conquest era when a dense rural population cultivated the land intensively. Warfare, forced labour drafts and diseases which accompanied the Spanish conquest, devastated the area. Many of the terraced zones have not been cultivated for centuries, and are now used merely as rough pasture.

these changes were positive, representing improvement and enlightenment. For the indigenous population, however, the changes were more difficult to interpret. From the viewpoint of most of the indigenous leaders, the Spanish and Portuguese conquests were disastrous. The conquest removed their power and their civilization, and replaced it with a cruelly imposed foreign culture. To a few indigenous leaders, however, and to most of the Indian population, the arrival of the Spaniards and Portuguese was little more than the replacement of one group of harsh rulers by another. Indeed, in the conquest of the Inca Empire some of the tribes which earlier had been conquered by the Incas helped the Spaniards to overthrow Inca rule. The full horror of the Spanish conquest did not become apparent until rather later, when millions of Indians died from European diseases.

By the eighteenth century the most destructive phase of the colonial period was over. Considering South America as a whole, we would argue that there has been a positive balance of development since then. In other words, taking all factors into account and viewing changes in the long term, we believe that there has been a general net improvement in the conditions for human life. There are, however, major differences between social and economic factors, political factors and environmental factors, and so we discuss each of these groups separately.

Social and economic factors

The improvement in the conditions for human life since the eighteenth century is most obvious in terms of health. There has been a general rise in life expectancy, a major decline in infant mortality, and a reduction in the incidence of infectious diseases. The health of the South American population is still considerably worse than that of European or North American populations. Nevertheless, few would deny that steady progress has been made over the last two centuries, and particularly since the 1940s. There have been smaller, but still very significant, improvements in the provision of education and in general levels of literacy, though, again,

South America continues to lag far behind most European and North American countries. The progress made in health and education has been associated with major improvements in physical infrastructure. There has been wider provision of clean drinking water, drainage, sewerage, electricity supply, access roads and street paving, and for a small minority at least, telephones and international telecommunications as well. Particularly since 1950, networks of paved roads, bus and truck transport services, airports and airline services have been created to link the main towns and cities in most South American countries. Several major cities and ports have also been equipped with deep-water shipping berths, large warehousing complexes and major international airports. International communications have certainly become much easier.

The widespread improvements in public services, in transport and communications, and in levels of health and education, have been paralleled by economic growth. Again, most of South America lags far behind most of Europe and North America in absolute wealth, but the percentage rates of growth over the last fifty years are broadly similar. South America remains behind, largely because the whole process of economic growth started later, and from a lower initial base. South America is also different because of the more unequal distribution of the benefits of growth among its population. The very uneven distribution of income and wealth among the population of South America is paralleled by huge inequalities in the distribution of public services, and in access to work opportunities. Overall, therefore, the most obvious negative feature of South American development is its unequal distribution. Indeed, while living conditions have certainly improved for the wealthiest third of the population in all South American countries over the last fifty years, in most countries conditions have not improved very much for the poorest third of the population. Many of the poor have actually suffered a long-term worsening of their living and working conditions. The benefits of 'development' have simply passed them by.

Growth in social and economic inequalities and a widespread failure to improve the living conditions of the very poor have not been the only negative features accompanying the substantial economic growth in South America since the 1930s. Many South American economies, and particularly those of the southern half of the continent, have suffered from extremely rapid inflation, with prices sometimes increasing by several hundred per cent per annum. Major balance of payments problems have also arisen in most South American countries because they have failed to produce sufficient food or fuel for their own needs, and have had to rely on expensive imports. Such imports have often been financed by heavy borrowing from abroad, leading to the problem of long-term debts. Almost all the South American countries now have massive international debts, particularly to banks in North America and Western Europe. The need to repay these debts, or at least to pay interest on the loans, is a major financial burden, and means that the countries often cannot afford to import much-needed equipment and raw materials. Furthermore, the pressure exerted by the international banks, combined with other pressures from foreign governments and multinational companies reduces the South American governments' capacity for self-reliance. In this way, an increased dependence on foreign countries has often accompanied the economic development of South

America. The governments have tended to rely very heavily on foreign rather than local resources.

Political factors

While growing social and economic inequalities and the continuation of poverty are the most obvious negative features of South American development, the continent also has a very bad record in terms of politics and human rights. Political independence, which was generally gained in the early nineteenth century, meant little more than a change of exploitative leaders. The direct link with Spain and Portugal was broken, but the main forms of exploitation remained and in some cases were actually increased after Independence. The wars of independence also strengthened the power of the army and paved the way for frequent army intervention in political affairs. Most of the South American countries have had military dictatorships for various periods since Independence. Between periods of military dictatorship, countries have also had elected governments. Both types of government have tended to be unstable. Elected governments have the threat of military take-over. Military rule is often unstable because it lacks the support of all groups within the army, and one army general will seize power from another. There are, however, two cases of very stable governments, the military dictatorships of General Alfredo Stroessner, who has been President of Paraguay since 1954, and of General Augusto Pinochet, who has been President of Chile since 1973.

The history of political instability and frequency of dictatorships has been accompanied by corruption and incompetence in government. Instability tends to encourage these, because many individuals try to grab what they can before losing their positions, and because staff have little time to get to know their jobs. Dictatorships also tend to encourage corruption because those who hold power take advantage of a situation where there is little public control. They also encourage incompetence because administrators and planners are often chosen more on the basis of friendship and political support than on the basis of ability.

South America is notable for the violence and abuse of human rights associated with politics. For example, when the elected government of President Salvador Allende in Chile was overthrown by the army in 1973, there were thousands of deaths. Torture was used on a large scale and there were other abuses of human rights which led to tens of thousands of Chileans leaving for other countries as political refugees. The suffering which occurred in Chile is just one well-known example of violence and abuse of human rights in South America. Over 220,000 people have died in the violence associated with political events in Colombia since the late 1940s, and there have been similar, but smaller-scale, happenings in other countries of the continent.

Overall, although we can speak of political change in South America, it is difficult to speak of political development, if we assume that development implies a general improvement. The continent seems caught in a tradition of rule by, and for, the better-off minority of the population. Even elected governments often reach power only by tampering with the electoral system, for example by rigging the votes. The result is that many people do not bother to vote, especially the poorest

Fig. 7.2 Military and civilian governments in South America, January 1988.

people in the rural areas. The powerful minority in the country benefits from the government, and the interests and problems of the poorer majority of the population are neglected.

The way that government is run in South America (Fig. 7.2) has an impact on the geography of the continent. Whether a government has been elected or has taken power by force, it tends to focus on a single individual. One leader, usually the President, with the help of his closest friends, will take all the major decisions of government. Ministries and other government agencies operate in the same way, so that all aspects of government, even if they concern the country's remotest provinces, are heavily centralized. The result is the concentration of government power and activity around the President and his ministers, in the capital city. This has, in turn, increased the migration to the capital city and encouraged the location of offices and factories there. The primacy of cities like Lima, Santiago, Buenos Aires and Caracas, has therefore been encouraged by the concentration of central government in that single location, and by the need for businessmen to work where they have easy access to government information. At the same time, regional and local authorities have tended to be very weak and this has reduced the development possibilities of smaller cities and of peripheral regions.

The weakness of the electoral system in South America has been to the disadvantage of the poorest social groups. The fact that poor people can vote is no help in countries where there are few elections, or where election results may be rigged. Throughout South America there is still widespread discrimination against the Negro and Indian populations. These groups are generally very poor and they usually work as servants, labourers or peasant farmers. Although there is no legally-enforced racial separation as in South Africa, the blacks and Indians are concentrated in

123

the poorest rural and urban neighbourhoods, and in the lowest-paid occupations. So far, there has been little sign of any effective political movement to improve their situation, and there seems little chance of such a movement in the near future.

The power of the armed forces in the governments of many South American countries has often led to large sums of public money being spent on the purchase of arms, and on the payment of fairly high wages to the military. This in turn has reduced the money available for other needs, such as education, roads and irrigation. Even more worrying is that the political and military rivalry between various South American countries has hindered economic integration between countries. Rivalry has prevented the success of such international organizations as the Latin American Free Trade Association (LAFTA) and the Andean Pact. Competition between countries has been a far stronger force than collaboration. It has led to the establishment of many uneconomic industrial projects, like steelworks, which lack good access either to raw materials or to markets. Competition has also delayed the linking of the various national road and railway networks into a good international transport system.

Environmental factors

In South America today, there is certainly a growing concern for the environment: for the conservation of natural resources, flora and fauna, and the reduction of pollution. Some steps have been taken to reduce soil erosion and deforestation. Energy resources are being used more efficiently, and moves have been made to establish national parks and nature reserves. The Pacific countries of South America were world leaders in extending their fishing limits to 200 miles, partly at least because of a concern that North American and Japanese fishing vessels were exhausting fish stocks. Venezuela and Ecuador have played an important role in the negotiations with other oil producers to reduce world oil consumption by limiting production and pushing up prices. Brazil has been a world leader in the use of alcohol from sugar-cane as a fuel for motor vehicles, in the place of petrol. In the 1970s Brazil also started many hydroelectric power projects and a large nuclear energy programme to reduce dependence on imported oil. Each of these major initiatives, however, could have been motivated more for reasons of national security and self-interest than for reasons of resource conservation.

Many critics would argue that the measures taken to conserve resources in South America are simply too little, and too late. Large tracts of the continent, particularly in the Andean Highlands and in North-East Brazil, have been severely affected by deforestation and soil erosion, leading to problems of flood, drought, and continuing loss of soil fertility. Large areas which were once productive farmland are now agriculturally useless, and this has accelerated migration to the continent's major cities. In turn, the cities have been increasingly blighted by traffic congestion and air pollution. This has produced an environment which is damaging to the physical and mental health of many of the urban population, and particularly of the poorer urban dwellers living in the crowded inner cities.

Fig. 7.3 The Montgomery bauxite mine near the town of Linden (formerly Mackenzie) in Guyana. The bauxite layer is just to the right and above the rail tracks. It is buried beneath 20 to 45 metres of overburden which is stripped and dumped (left) with a dramatic effect on the environment.

In parts of South America human activity has had a devastating impact on the environment, which has caused serious problems for human occupation of the areas. An example is North-East Brazil, where many of the smaller towns were literally ransacked by starving peasants in the 1970s. These people became destitute because their farm plots were too small and lacked the supplies of irrigation water necessary for the crops to survive the frequent droughts. As a result of both the land tenure and climatic situation, soil erosion accelerated, destroying all hope of a livelihood for thousands of people. At the same time, in the major cities of the continent, deaths from heart attacks, lung cancer and other diseases of 'modern society' have been increasing rapidly. This is especially true in Caracas where air pollution and problems of congestion are particularly severe. Many small areas of the continent have been ruined by pollution and mining waste (Fig. 7.3). One spectacular example is the zone around the non-ferrous metal refinery of La Oroya in central highland Peru, where almost all vegetation within a 5-kilometre radius has been poisoned (Fig. 7.4). Even more worrying from a global, environmental viewpoint is the impact of large-scale forest clearance, lumbering and agricultural colonization on the Amazon basin. Although this area is still largely forest and remains the world's largest forest reserve, clearance is proceeding at an increasing rate. The forest is being destroyed on various fronts, both westward and northward from the more populated areas of Brazil, and eastward from the Andean Highlands. This has led to serious concern over soil erosion, the destruction of natural habitats, and changes in drainage patterns and climate.

Despite the many environmental problems, South American governments can claim that, overall, the environment has not deteriorated to the extent that it did in Western Europe during the nineteenth and early twentieth century, or to the extent, for example, that it has deteriorated in the areas fringing the Sahara Desert during the twentieth century. South America, by world standards, is still a fairly empty and sparsely-populated continent. Its reserves of unused and under-used natural resources are still quite significant. Major improvements have been made in the conditions for human life in many rural areas, through the control

Fig. 7.4 La Oroya in the Andes of central Peru. The smelters shown in the photograph have severely polluted the river and killed all plants on the surrounding hillsides.

Fig. 7.5 Part of the central business district of São Paulo in Brazil. The high density of tall buildings and the urban motorways suggest not only the congestion and air pollution which characterize such large cities, but also the concentration of economic and social activities which attract new migrants to the city.

of tropical diseases and through the provision of roads, electricity and water supply. At the same time, living conditions are generally not so bad in the towns and cities as to deter rural–urban migration. Indeed, many would argue that the higher availability of goods, services and employment opportunities in the cities far outweighs the significance of such mainly urban hazards as air pollution and increased road-accident rates (Fig. 7.5).

There is obvious scope for improving the environment in South America, concentrating, for example, on reforestation, pollution control, and the encouragement of crops and agricultural practices which safeguard soil fertility. It is unlikely, however, that such policies could significantly improve the environment, without a major redistribution of income and wealth in the continent, and without a shift in national policy towards increased national self-reliance. The current environmental problems are largely the result of the continent's stark combination of considerable wealth for a minority, and poverty for a majority, and also the result of penetration by foreign interests which are not particularly concerned with the long-term consequences of their actions. The grossly unequal distribution of land encourages careless land use by the wealthy land owners and over-intensive land use by the poorest smallholders. Foreign companies are equally damaging because of their 'get rich quick' attitude to the exploitation of natural resources.

The mixture of exploitative large-scale production and intensive small-scale production underlies much of the inefficiency and waste in South American resource use. Only a political change towards more stable and democratic government, together with a major redistribution of income, wealth and access to agricultural land to help the poor, can produce the conditions necessary for less destructive resource use. Regrettably, however, it is difficult to see how such changes will come about. The immediate future of South America seems to offer little more than a continuation of high levels of social and economic inequality, gradual improvement in infrastructure, and moderate economic growth. This is likely to be combined with a continuing reliance on imports, loans, technology and investments from the world's richest countries, and with relatively exploitative and wasteful use of national resources. For some this will represent 'development', but for others it will seem nothing more than the reinforcement of national underdevelopment.

Further reading

Most of these books are available in paperback.

General texts on development studies and world development issues:

Armstrong, W. and McGee, T. G. (1985) *Theatres of accumulation: studies in Asian and Latin American urbanization*, Methuen, London.

Bromley, R. (ed.) (1985) *Planning for small enterprises in Third World cities*, Pergamon, Oxford.

Caldwell, M. (1977) *The wealth of some nations*, Zed Press, London.

Drakakis-Smith, D. (1987) *The Third World city*, Methuen, London.

Edwards, C. (1985) *The fragmented world*, Methuen, London.

Foley, G. (1981) *The energy question* (2nd edn), Penguin, Harmondsworth.

George, S. (1984) *Ill fares the land*, Institute for Policy Studies, Washington DC.

Gilbert, A. and Gugler, J. (1982) *Cities, poverty and development*, Oxford University Press, Oxford.

GJW Government Relations with Peter Stephenson (1981) *Handbook of world development: the guide to the Brandt Report*, Longman, London.

Harris, N. (1983) *Of bread and guns: the world economy in crisis*, Pelican, Harmondsworth.

Harrison, P. (1981) *Inside the Third World* (2nd edn), Penguin, Harmondsworth.

Hayter, T. (1981) *The creation of world poverty: an alternative view to the Brandt Report*, Pluto Press, London.

Inter-American Development Bank (1987) *Economic and social progress in the Americas* (annual publication), Inter-American Development Bank, Washington DC.

Jenkins, R. (1987) *Transnational corporations and uneven development*, Methuen, London.

Kidron, M. and Segal, R. (1984) *New state of the world atlas*, Pan, London.

Kitching, G. (1982) *Development and underdevelopment in historical perspective*, Methuen, London.

Mabogunje, A. L. (1980) *The development process: a spatial perspective*, Hutchinson, London.

Redclift, M. (1984) *Development and the environmental crisis*, Methuen, London.

Reitsma, H. A. and Kleinpenning, J. M. G. (1985) *The Third World in perspective*, Rowman and Allanheld, Totowa, NJ.

Santos, M. (1979) *The shared space: the two circuits of the urban economy in underdeveloped countries*, Methuen, London.

Smith, D. M. (1979) *Where the grass is greener: living in an unequal world*, Penguin, Harmondsworth.

World Bank (1987) *World development report 1987* (annual publication), Oxford University Press, New York.

Geography texts on Latin America, South America, and Brazil:

Blakemore, H. and Smith, C. T. (eds) (1983) *Latin America: geographical perspectives* (2nd edn), Methuen, London.

Dickenson, J. P. (1983) *Brazil*, Longman, London.

Henshall, J. D. and Momsen, R. P. (1974) *A geography of Brazilian development*, Bell and Hyman, London.

Morris, A. (1981) *South America* (2nd edn), Hodder and Stoughton, London.

Odell, P. R. and Preston, D. A. (1978) *Economies and societies of Latin America: a geographical interpretation* (2nd edn), Wiley, Chichester.

Studies of specific themes and countries in South America:

Branford, S. and Glock, O. (1985) *The last frontier: fighting over land in the Amazon*, Zed Press, London.

Burbach, R. and Flynn, P. (1980) *Agribusiness in the Americas*, Monthly Review Press, New York.

Cardoso, F. H. and Faletto, E. (1979) *Dependency and development in Latin America*, University of California Press, Berkeley.

Davis, S. (1977) *Victims of the miracle: Development and the Indians of Brazil*, Cambridge University Press, Cambridge.

Dunkerley, J. (1984) *Rebellion in the veins: political struggle in Bolivia 1952–1982*, Verso, London.

Latin-America Bureau (1980) *Paraguay: power game*, LAB, London.

— (1984) *Guyana: fraudulent revolution*, LAB, London.

Lombardi, C. L. and Lombardi, J. V. (1983) *Latin American history: a teaching atlas*, University of Wisconsin Press, Madison.

Pendle, G. (1976) *A history of Latin America* (revised edn), Penguin, Harmondsworth.

Perlman, J. E. (1979) *The myth of marginality: urban poverty and politics in Rio de Janeiro*, University of California Press, Berkeley.

Reid, M. (1985) *Peru: paths to poverty*, Latin America Bureau, London.

Sanchez-Albornoz, N. (1984) *The population of Latin America*, University of California Press, Berkeley.

Stein, S. J. and Stein, B. H. (1970) *The colonial heritage of Latin America*, Oxford University Press, New York.

Stone, R. D. (1985) *Dreams of Amazonia*, Penguin, Harmondsworth.